朗文
读名著

每周读一部英文名著

The Secret Garden

秘密花园

原著：［美］F. H. 伯内特（F. H. Burnett）
改写：［英］S. 乌尔斯坦（S. Ullstein）
翻译：张艳敏

中国出版集团公司
中国对外翻译出版有限公司
PEARSON Longman

图书在版编目（CIP）数据

秘密花园：英汉对照/(美)伯内特(Burnett, F. H.)著；(英)乌尔斯坦(Ullstein, S.)改写；张艳敏译．—北京：中国对外翻译出版有限公司, 2011. 7

（朗文经典．读名著 学英语）

书名原文：The Secret Garden

ISBN 978-7-5001-3129-8

I. ①秘… II. ①伯… ②乌… ③张… III. ①英语—汉语—对照读物 ②儿童文学—长篇小说—美国—现代 IV. ①H319. 4：I

中国版本图书馆CIP数据核字(2011)第125360号

著作权合同登记：图字01-2011-7043号

出版发行 / 中国对外翻译出版有限公司
地　　址 / 北京市西城区车公庄大街甲4号物华大厦六层
电　　话 / (010)68359827　68359303(发行部)　68359719(编辑部)
邮　　编 / 100044
传　　真 / (010)68357870
电子邮箱 / book@ctpc. com. cn
网　　址 / http://www. ctpc. com. cn　http://www. aitbook. com

出版策划 / 张高里
责任编辑 / 刘香玲　宋德伟
封面设计 / 张亚群
排　　版 / 竹叶图文
印　　刷 / 保定市中画美凯印刷有限公司
经　　销 / 新华书店

规　　格 / 820×1050mm　1/32
印　　张 / 6.25
版　　次 / 2012年1月第1版
印　　次 / 2012年1月第1次

ISBN 978-7-5001-3129-8　定价：12. 90元

中国对外翻译出版有限公司

Copyright Notice

致学习者

每周读一部英文名著，7天快速提升阅读力！

近年来，随着英语素质教育越来越受到重视，教师、学生和家长都认识到进行大量原版英语阅读对于学好英语的重要性，国家教育部颁布的《英语课程标准》也对学生课外英语阅读提出了更高的标准和要求。为全面提升英语学习者的阅读能力，给英语学习者提供一个原汁原味的英语学习环境，中国对外翻译出版有限公司隆重推出“朗文经典·读名著 学英语”阅读系列。

本系列丛书针对中国英语学习者的学习习惯，采用中英文对照编排的形式，通过典雅精美的译文、准确实用的注释、精心设置的栏目等，扫除了读者的阅读障碍，帮助读者在了解原著内容的同时提升英语综合能力。丛书根据词汇控制理论，共分为9个级别，为不同水平的读者提供符合其词汇量水平的优秀读本。

熟读简易英文名著，

学会用简单的词语表达丰富的意境！

无论是口语，还是写作，

你的英文表达力都将一鸣惊人！

阅读指南

READING GUIDE

❶内容简介，提前预热

简要介绍该书的作家生平、故事情节、作品中人物的性格特征及作品的影响力等。让读者在开始阅读之前对作品有一个大概的了解，这有利于提升读者的阅读兴趣。

❷词汇控制，难度分级

外籍专家根据朗文公司制定的“词汇控制”原则，在简写每部作品时都进行了严格控制，为不同水平的读者提供了与其词汇量相对应的优秀读本。“朗文经典”根据词汇控制理论，共分为9个级别：

1000词；1200词；1500词；1800词；2000词；2200词；2500词；2800词；3000词。

Introduction

R D Blackmore

Richard Doddridge Blackmore was born in 1825, the son of a **Church of England priest**. He went to school in Tiverton, which is where we meet John Ridd in the first chapter of this book.

Blackmore went to Exeter College, Oxford, and then studied law. He practised as a lawyer in the courts for a few years, but poor health forced him to leave London, and he started growing flowers, fruit and vegetables for the market. At the same time, he wrote poetry, not very successfully. His first novel, *Clara Vaughan*, was much more successful when it appeared in 1864.

His historical novel *Lorna Doone* appeared in 1869. It was not a great success when it first came out in three **volumes**. Some people liked the way the hero, John Ridd, was presented on his Exmoor farm, the way his love of the country became clear. They spoke to others about the book, its exciting adventures and its tender love story, and so more people read it. It became a **classic**, although neither the writer nor the booksellers expected it. And it is still a well-loved classic, often used today as material for films and television.

It was partly an accident that the novel became a **"best-seller"**. A young member of the company which had produced

❸读前问题，引导思路

针对每章（篇）的故事情节提出若干个问题，通过问题线索引导读者的阅读思路，抓住阅读重点，从而提升读者的阅读效率。

CHAPTER 1

The Doones

杜恩家族

· QUESTIONS BEFORE READING ·

- There were three people in the carriage. Who were they?
- What had happened to John Ridd's father?
- Who were Annie and Lizzie?
- Why did John teach himself to use a gun? (Because...)

❹名著简写，原汁原味

外籍英语专家根据原著精心简写，用词简洁，句型简单，既保留了原著精彩的故事情节，又保证了语言的原汁原味和通俗易懂，易于提升读者阅读的成就感。

My name is John Ridd. My home is in Oare, a village in a part of England called Somerset. My father was a farmer. The farm came to him from his father; it had been our farm for hundreds of years. I went to school in Tiverton. I learnt a little at school, but I left school early.

This is how I left school on the twenty-ninth of November, 1673.

We came out of school at five o'clock. A long line of horses was coming down the road with soldiers **guarding** them. The horses were carrying goods. They were being guarded because it was said that Tom Faggus was near and might steal the goods. Tom Faggus was my **cousin**. He was well known as a **highwayman**.

We all ran to the gate to see the soldiers pass.

Just then a man with horses came round the corner.

"Have any of you seen John Ridd?" he asked.

The man was John Fry; he was a **servant** at our home.

I went forward and spoke to him. "Why have you come at this time, John?" I asked, "School doesn't end until next month. There is a month more of school."

❺英汉对照，扫除障碍

全书英文部分全部配有参考译文。译文除了能帮助读者更好地理解作品外，还可以帮助读者通过英汉文字的对比，了解两种语言不同的表达方式，提升语感和翻译写作能力。

1685年查理二世死后，民众更加不满，因为他的弟弟，新国王詹姆斯二世是罗马天主教徒。很多人支持蒙茅斯公爵而不是詹姆斯当国王。蒙茅斯是查理二世的儿子，但是查理国王和他的母亲可能没有结婚。蒙茅斯的支持者们开始为他从海外归来取代詹姆斯做安排。但是这些人动作太慢，蒙茅斯和他的顾问智囊们又太急躁。公爵在多塞特郡的莱姆里吉斯登陆，此时距查理的死只有4个月。他的支持者们能够为他召集的队伍只是那些没有受过训练的乡下人，就像本书中约翰·里德描述的那样。在不到一个月的时间里，这支"队伍"就被詹姆斯的正规军在萨默塞特郡的塞奇高沼区消灭了。蒙茅斯被处死，他的支持者们也在法官杰弗里斯操控下的"血腥巡回裁判庭"受审。

Roman Catholic 罗马天主教徒

forces *n.* 武装力量，军队

regular army 正规军

marsh *n.* 沼泽，湿地

Bloody Assizes 血腥巡回裁判庭

埃克斯穆尔

埃克斯穆尔位于英国西部萨默塞特郡和德文郡之间。其大部分是高地，海拔超过500米。东西长约34公里，南北宽约20公里。地势较高的部分寸木不生，只有低矮的灌木，岩石和沼泽。其间有美丽的峡谷，本书所描述的奥阿拉村就位于其中一个峡谷，今天你仍然可以找到这个村子。从那里出发才能寻见两条小溪谷，分别叫兰克库姆和霍克姆库姆，在这两条美丽的溪谷之间就是布莱克默尔所描述的杜恩峡谷。

❻难词注释，积累词汇

书中对部分难词和重点词进行了汉语注释，这有利于保证读者在阅读英文时的连贯性，并借助于上下文更好地理解和运用这些词汇。

❼美文佳句，日积月累

章节中出现的美文佳句，值得学习者反复研读、背诵和模仿。

Language Points to Remember
好句好段记心上

1. Just then a man with horses came round the corner.
   就在这时，一个牵马的男人从拐弯处出现了。
2. We left Tiverton early in the morning.
   一大早我们就离开了蒂弗顿。
3. The mist lay thick on the moor so that we could not see beyond our horses' heads.
   沼泽上浓雾弥漫，我们都无法看清马头前面的东西。
4. They were heavy, big men, carrying guns.
   他们个个五大三粗，手里都拿着枪。
5. All the lands were owned by these two men, and each received one half of the money got from them.
   所有这些土地都归这两个人所有，这些土地上的收入由他们平分。
6. I was only a boy when my father died; but I knew that my time would come.
   我父亲死的时候我还是个孩子，但是我知道复仇的日子总会到来。

目 录
CONTENTS

The Secret Garden

Introduction

Frances Hodgson Burnett

Frances Hodgson was born in Manchester, England, in 1849. Her father was successful as a **dealer** in metal goods, but he died while Frances was still very young. The family continued to **deal** in metal goods, but more and more of their trade was with the southern states of America. The American Civil War, between the northern states and some southern states (1861—65), ended badly for the southern states and for the Hodgson company. The Hodgsons went to the United States and lived in the state of Tennessee.

They were very poor until Frances had some success as a writer from 1866, when she was seventeen years old.

In 1873, Frances Hodgson married Dr Swan Burnett. Her name was already known to many readers, so Mrs Frances Burnett kept the "Hodgson" in her name as a writer.

She had great success with her novel *Little Lord Fauntleroy* in 1886. Learned people now think that this story of an American boy who becomes an English **lord** is not good because it plays too much on the reader's feelings. But thousands of people enjoyed it.

简介

弗朗西丝·霍奇森·伯内特

弗朗西丝1849年生于英格兰曼彻斯特。她的父亲经营五金制品，颇为成功，当她父亲去世时，弗朗西丝年纪尚幼。她们家继续经营五金制品，但是越来越多的生意是和美国南部诸州进行的。美国北部各州和南部某些州之间爆发了“南北战争”(1861—1865)，并以南部各州的战败而告终，这也给霍奇森公司带来了厄运。这一家人前往美国，并在田纳西州定居。

dealer
n. 业者，商人

deal
v. 经营，从事

他们家境贫苦，直到1866年，17岁的弗朗西丝写作取得一定成功后，家境才有所好转。

弗朗西丝·霍奇森1873年和斯万·伯内特医生结婚。因为她在许多读者中已经颇有名气，所以弗朗西丝·伯内特夫人作为作家，在名字中保留了“霍奇森”。

弗朗西丝于1886年出版的小说《方特勒罗伊小爵爷》取得了巨大成功。如今饱学之士并不看好这个关于一个美国小男孩成为一个英国爵爷的故事，因为它过于煽情，但在当时有成千上万的人喜欢它。

lord
n. 领主，君主；贵族

The Secret Garden came out in 1909. It was written for children, but older people enjoy it because it shows the writer's surprising understanding of children, even when she herself was sixty years old.

Frances Hodgson Burnett died in 1924 in Long Island, USA.

The Secret Garden

The story begins in India at a time when very many British people lived there. They worked in **government**, in the army, on the railways and in trade. They were not all like the father and mother of Mary in this story, but many of them had plenty of Indian servants, and sometimes the European mothers did not give enough time and care to their own children. The hot season was not good for Europeans, and there were illnesses that the doctors did not know much about. That is how Mary became an **unhealthy**, rather **nasty** child.

England would seem a strange country after the India that Mary knew. And the Yorkshire **moors** would be even stranger. They are cold in winter. The wind blows strongly over them, with very few trees to stop it. You don't see many houses on the high moors, and the rough grass is all right for sheep but not for cows or other farm animals. The Yorkshire people believe it is very healthy, but an unhappy little child from India wouldn't think so at first.

《秘密花园》出版于1909年，它本是儿童读物，但是年纪大一些的人也喜欢读，因为它表明了作者对于儿童有着惊人的理解，即使当时她自己已经60岁了。

1924年，弗朗西丝·霍奇森·伯内特于美国长岛离世。

《秘密花园》

government
n. 政府

故事发生在印度，当时很多英国人住在那里。这些人或在政府、军队里，或在铁路、贸易界工作。他们并不都像书中玛丽的父母，但是其中许多人雇佣了大量的印度仆人，而且有时欧洲母亲很少陪伴孩子，对他们也照顾不周。炎热的气候对欧洲人不利，那里还有医生们所知甚少的疾病。玛丽就是这样成为一个体弱多病、性情乖戾的女孩。

unheathy
adj. 不健康的
nasty
adj. 讨厌的
moor
n. 草甸

玛丽在熟悉了印度的生活之后，英格兰就显得陌生了，而约克郡的草甸子则更为奇异了。那里冬季寒冷，树木稀疏，挡不住劲吹的狂风。凸起的草甸上房屋很少，粗糙的野草对于羊群还尚可食用，但对于牛和别的家畜就不行了。约克郡人认为这非常有益健康，但是一个来自印度而且并不快乐的小孩起初是不会这样想的。

CHAPTER 1
There Is No One Left

没剩下一个人

· Questions before Reading ·

- Who took care of Mary in India?
- What happened to her father and mother?
- Why did no one care about Mary? (Because . . .)

Mary Lennox was born in India. Her mother and father were from England, but they lived in India because her father worked there. Mary's mother was very beautiful. She had many friends and she liked to go out with them. She was always with her friends. She had not really wanted a child at all. Mary's father was often out, too, because he worked very hard. So Mary did not see her mother or father very often. Servants **took care of** her. They did everything to please her and to stop her crying.

Mary was a thin, ugly baby who was often ill. She did not get better as she grew bigger. She was always a thin, unhealthy child. Because the servants always did what she wanted, she was not at all a nice child. She thought only about herself. No one loved Mary, and Mary loved no one.

One very hot morning when Mary was nine years old, a new servant came to wake her. Mary was **cross** because she wanted the servant whom she knew, not a new one.

The woman looked frightened, but Mary's own servant did not come. Later, Mary was left alone. It was a Strange morning. No one told her what to do, so she went into the garden to play.

玛丽·伦诺克斯出生在印度。她父母来自英国，但由于她的父亲在印度工作，所以他们家住在印度。玛丽的母亲是个美人，朋友众多，她喜欢和他们出去玩。她总是和朋友们在一起，她根本不想要孩子。玛丽的父亲也经常外出，因为他工作很努力。因此玛丽很少见到她的父母。她由仆人们照管，他们千方百计哄她高兴，不让她哭。

take care of
照顾

玛丽是个又瘦又丑的小孩，经常生病。她逐渐长大了，但身体并没变好。她一直都是一个体弱多病的孩子。因为仆人们老是顺着她，她可不是容易相处的女孩子。她心里只有自己，谁都不爱玛丽，玛丽也不爱任何人。

玛丽九岁那年，一个非常炎热的清晨，一位新女佣来叫她起床。玛丽生气了，因为她想要那个她熟悉的女佣，而不是新来的。

cross
adj. 生气的

这名女佣看来吓坏了，可是玛丽自己的那个女佣还是没来。后来，就剩玛丽自己一个人了。那真是一个奇怪的上午，没有人告诉她该干什么，所以她就

She played with flowers and made a little garden of her own. She was cross because she did not know why she was alone. Something was not right.

Later she heard her mother talking and then she knew what was not right. Many people in the house were ill, and some had died. No one thought about Mary. No one wanted her, and she was sad. She was frightened, too. She went to her room. She cried and then she slept for a long time. When she woke up, the house was very quiet.

"Perhaps the sickness has gone," she thought. "Perhaps everyone is better. Now someone will come and look for me."

But no one came. She waited, but the house was still very quiet. Suddenly she heard footsteps outside her room, and two men came in.

"Barney!" the first man cried. "There's a child in here! A child alone! In a place like this! Who is she?"

"I am Mary Lennox," the little girl said crossly. "I went to sleep when everyone was ill, and I have just **woken up**. Why does no one come? Why didn't they remember me?"

"Poor little girl!" said the man called Barney. "There is no one left who could remember you."

And so Mary learnt that her father and mother were dead. The servants had all run away, and no one thought about the little girl who was left alone in the house. She was not a nice child, and no one **cared about** her.

到花园里去玩了。她摆弄各种花草，给自己弄了一个小花园。她很不高兴，因为她不明白为什么只有自己一个人，一定出事了。

后来她听见她母亲说话，才知道出了什么事。宅子里许多人生了病，有些人已经死了。谁也没有想到玛丽，也没人理她，她感到很伤心，也很害怕，她回到自己的屋里，哭了一会儿，然后睡了很长时间。等她醒来时，宅子里一片寂静。

“也许疫病已经过去了，”她想，“也许大家都好转了。现在总会有人来找我了。”

可还是没有人来。她等了又等，宅子里还是悄无声息。突然间她听到房间外面有脚步声，接着两个男人进了她的房间。

“巴尼！”第一个人叫道，“这儿有个孩子！就她一个人！在这种地方！她是谁呀？”

“我叫玛丽·伦诺克斯，”小女孩生气地说，“大家都生病的时候，我睡着了，现在刚睡醒。为什么没有人来？他们为什么把我忘了？”

wake up
醒来

“可怜的小姑娘！”那个叫巴尼的人说，“能够记得你的人一个也不在了。”

现在，玛丽才知道她的父母都死了。仆人们都逃走了，谁也没有想起独自留在宅子里的小姑娘。她性情不讨人喜欢，因此谁都不关心她。

care about
关心

Language Points to Remember
好句好段记心上

1. Because the servants always did what she wanted, she was not at all a nice child.
   因为仆人们老是顺着她，她可不是容易相处的女孩子。

2. The servants had all run away, and no one thought about the little girl who was left alone in the house.
   仆人们都逃走了，谁也没有想起独自留在宅子里的小姑娘。

CHAPTER 2
Mary Goes to England
玛丽到英国去了

· Questions before Reading ·

- Who was Mary's uncle?
- Who met Mary in London?
- What was the matter with Mr Craven? (He was . . . , and his wife . . .)

Mary had no family in India, so she went home to England to live with her uncle, Mr Archibald Craven. Mary had never been to England and she knew nothing about her uncle, who was her mother's brother. She was told that he lived in a big old house in the country, and that he was a **hunchback**. This frightened Mary. She thought, too, about Yorkshire, and the place where she was going to live. She knew only that it was called Misselthwaite **Manor**, and that Yorkshire was in the north of England.

One of Mr Craven's servants, Mrs Medlock, met Mary in London. She was a fat woman with a red face and little black eyes. Mary did not like her at all, and Mrs Medlock did not seem to like Mary very much.

During the journey to Yorkshire by train, Mary sat silently and looked out of the window. She had nothing to read, and she looked ugly and cross. Her black dress made her look colourless and ill. Since her mother and father's death she had begun to think strange thoughts. She had begun to wonder why she always felt so alone. Other children seemed to be part

玛丽在印度没有亲人，所以她去到英国和她的舅舅，阿尔博尔德·克雷文一起生活。玛丽从来没有到过英国，对舅舅，这位母亲的兄弟，也一无所知。有人告诉她说，舅舅住在乡下一所古老的大庄园里，还说他是个驼背，这让玛丽很害怕。她还想到了要去住的约克郡。她只知道这宅子叫做米瑟斯韦特庄园，还知道约克郡在英格兰北部。

hunchback
n. 驼背

manor
n. 宅邸，庄园

克雷文先生的一位名叫梅德洛克太太的女佣到伦敦来接玛丽。她身材肥胖，面色绯红，长着一对小黑眼睛。玛丽一点也不喜欢她，而梅德洛克太太似乎也不太喜欢玛丽。

乘火车前往约克郡的途中，玛丽一言不发，看着窗外。她没有书可看，脸色不好，很不高兴的样子。她的黑色孝服使她看起来面无血色，一副病容。自从她父母去世以后，她就开始有了一些诡异的念头，她开始纳闷为什么自己总是感到这么孤独。别人家的孩子同父母在一起，像家庭的一部分。可是她自己，

of a family with their mothers and fathers; but even when her mother and father were alive, she had never seemed to be part of a family. She had had food and clothes and servants to take care of her, but no one had really loved her. She did not know that this was because she was not a nice child. She did not know that she was not nice.

Mrs Medlock had never seen a child who sat so still and did nothing. Mrs Medlock did not like Sitting quietly, so at last she said to Mary: "Do you know your uncle?"

"No," answered Mary.

"Didn't your father and mother talk about him?"

"No," said Mary again. Her father and mother had never talked to her about anything.

"Oh," said Mrs Medlock, and she was silent. Then she began again: "Do you know that you're going to a very strange place?" she asked.

Mary did not answer, and Mrs Medlock was surprised because the child was not interested in where she was going to live.

"The house is six hundred years old, and it's near the moor," she went on. "There are a hundred rooms, but most of them are **shut up** and are not used. There are big gardens round the house, and trees, and . . . " she stopped and then she said, "But there's nothing more."

Mary was always interested in new things, but she did not want people to know that she was interested, so she sat still.

"Well," said Mrs Medlock. "What do you think of it?"

即使父母在世的时候，也从来没有感觉像家庭的一员。她有吃有穿，有仆人照顾她，可没人真正爱过她。她并不明白这是因为她不好相处，她不知道自己是个不好相处的孩子。

梅德洛克太太从来没有见过一个孩子这样安静地坐着，无所事事。她自己不喜欢默默地坐着，因此她向玛丽问道："你认得你舅舅吗？"

"不认得。"玛丽答。

"难道你父母没有谈起过他吗？"

"没有。"玛丽说，她父母什么都没有对她提起过。

"噢，"梅德洛克太太沉默了一会儿，接着又说起来，"你知不知道你要到一个很奇怪的地方去？"她问道。

玛丽没有回答她，梅德洛克太太感到惊讶，因为这孩子毫不关心她要去生活的地方。

"那宅子已经有600年的历史了，离草甸子很近，"她继续说，"有100个房间，可是大多数房间都关着不用。宅子周围有许多大花园，有树，还有……"她停顿了一下，然后又说，"可是再没有别的东西了。"

shut up
关闭

玛丽对于新事物总是很有兴趣，但又不想让别人知道她感兴趣，所以她坐着，一句话也不说。

"嗯，你是怎么想的？"梅德洛克太太说。

"Nothing," Mary answered.

This made Mrs Medlock laugh. "Eh!" she said. "You're like a little old woman. Don't you care?"

"It isn't important whether I care or not," said Mary.

"You're right," said Mrs Medlock. "It isn't important. I don't know why you're coming to Misselthwaite Manor, but I'm sure that Mr Craven isn't going to **take** any **notice of** you. He never takes any notice of anyone. He's a strange man, and he's a hunchback. He was never happy until he was married."

Mary looked at Mrs Medlock carefully. She was surprised to think of a hunchback being married. Mrs Medlock was pleased that at last the child seemed to be interested in something.

"His wife was a sweet pretty woman," she said. "He loved her more than anything in the world. When she died—"

"Oh! Did she die?" Mary asked. Suddenly she felt sorry for Mr Craven.

"Yes, she died," Mrs Medlock answered. "And now he's as strange as ever. He's away most of the time; and when he is at Misselthwaite Manor, he stays in one part of the house and only his servant sees him."

It sounded like a story from a book, and it made Mary feel sad: a house with a hundred rooms—near a moor (and Mary did not know what a moor was)—a man who was a hunchback and who did not like people.

“我没有想法。”玛丽回答。

这使得梅德洛克太太笑了起来。“呃！”她说，“你像是个小老太太。你不关心吗？”

“我关不关心并不重要。”玛丽说。

“你说得对，”梅德洛克太太说，“是不重要。我不知道你为什么到米瑟斯韦特庄园来，但是我可以肯定克雷文先生不会留意到你。他对谁都漠不关心，他是个怪人，还是个驼背。他结婚以前一直没有感到过幸福。”

take notice of 注意到，关注，理会

玛丽仔细地地看了看梅德洛克太太。想到一个驼背人竟然结婚，她感到诧异。梅德洛克太太觉得高兴，因为那孩子好像终于对某件事情感兴趣了。

“他的夫人是一个又温柔、又漂亮的女人，”她说，“在世上，他最爱的就是她了。她死的时候——”

“噢！她死了吗？”玛丽问道，她突然为克雷文先生感到难过。

“对，她死了，”梅德洛克太太回答道，“现在克雷文先生又和过去一样古怪了。他大部分时间都不在，在米瑟斯韦特庄园的时候，他只待在宅子的一部分房间里，只有佣人才见得到他。”

这听起来真像是书里写的故事，让玛丽感到伤心：一座有100间房间的庄园——离草甸子很近（而玛丽还不明白草甸子是什么）——一个驼背的人，不喜欢和人来往。

Language Points to Remember
好句好段记心上

1. Mary had never been to England and she knew nothing about her uncle, who was her mother's brother.
   玛丽从来没有到过英国，对舅舅，这位母亲的兄弟，也一无所知。
2. She did not know that she was not nice.
   她不知道自己是个不好相处的孩子。
3. He never takes any notice of anyone.
   他对谁都漠不关心。

CHAPTER 3
Across the Moor
穿过草甸子

· Questions before Reading ·

- What do you call high land in Yorkshire where only rough grass grows?
- When is the moor pretty?

Mary slept for a long time. It was dark when she woke up.

"Wake up!" cried Mrs Medlock. "This is where we get out. Quickly! We've still got a long drive to the manor."

It was still raining. Mary was **wide** awake now. She wanted to see the strange place which Mrs Medlock had told her about.

"What is a moor?" she asked suddenly.

"Look out of the window in ten minutes' time and you'll see it," Mrs Medlock answered. "We have to drive five miles across the moor, but you won't see much because it's a dark night."

Mary did not ask any more questions. She sat and looked out of the window. First, they drove through a small town, and then they were out in the **open** country, where there were only trees and fields. Then the horses began to climb up a hill. There were no trees or fields now. Mary could see very little in the darkness.

"We're on the moor now," said Mrs Medlock.

The wind made a strange, low sound.

"It's . . . it's not the sea, is it?" asked Mary.

玛丽睡了很久。她醒来时天已经黑了。

“醒醒！”梅德洛克太太喊，“我们在这下车。快点！我们还要赶很长一段路才能到庄园呢。”

外面还在下雨，玛丽现在完全清醒了。她想看看梅德洛克太太给她讲的那个奇怪的地方。

wide
adv. 全部地，完全地

“草甸子是什么？”她忽然问。

“过10分钟你再向窗外看，你就会看见了，”梅德洛克太太回答道，“我们要穿过5英里的草甸子，可是天太黑，你不会看得太清楚。”

玛丽没有再问，她坐下来，望向车窗外边。马车先是穿过一座小镇，然后就驶入了旷野，只见树木和农田。然后马儿们开始爬坡。现在既没有树木，也没有农田了，黑暗中，玛丽几乎看不到什么东西。

open
adj. 空旷的

“我们现在到草甸子了。”梅德洛克太太说。

风吹过来，发出一种低沉的怪声。

“这……这不是大海吧？”玛丽问道。

"No, it's not," answered Mrs Medlock. "It isn't the sea and it isn't fields, nor is it mountains. It's just miles and miles of land where nothing grows except rough grass."

"It sounds like the sea now," said Mary.

"That's because of the wind," said Mrs Medlock. "It's a sad place, I think, but some people like it. It's very pretty in the spring when the flowers are out."

On and on they drove through the darkness. The road went **up and down**, and Mary felt that the journey would never end.

"I don't like it," she said. "I don't like it."

At last they stopped in front of a long, low house. Mary could see only one light in the whole house. Inside, she found herself in a large, dark room. She looked very small in her black coat, and she felt very small, too. Then Mrs Medlock took her to her room. They walked for a long time. At last Mrs Medlock said: "Well, here you are! This room and the next one are yours—and you must stay in them. Remember that!"

And so Mary began her life at Misselthwaite Manor, and she had never felt so cross and alone in her life. She was also rather **frightened**.

“不，这不是大海。”梅德洛克太太回答说，“这不是大海，不是田野，也不是山峦。这只是绵延好几英里的土地，除了荒草以外什么也不长。”

“现在听着像是大海。”玛丽说。

“那是因为在刮风，”梅德洛克太太说，“我觉得这是个荒凉之地，可是有些人喜欢它。春暖花开的时候，这地方很美。”

他们的马车在黑暗中走了又走，一会儿上坡，一会儿又下坡，玛丽觉得旅途永远也走不完。

up and down
上上下下

“我不喜欢这里，”她说，“我不喜欢这里。”

他们终于在一座又长又低的房子前面停了下来。整个房子，玛丽只看得见一盏灯光。进屋以后，她发现自己站在一个又大又暗的房间里。她穿着黑色外套的身形显得很矮小，而且她也感到自己很渺小。然后梅德洛克太太带她到自己的房间去，她们走了很长时间。终于梅德洛克太太说道：“好，到了！这间屋子，还有隔壁那间，都是你的——你必须待在这两间屋子里。记住！”

这样，玛丽开始了她在米瑟斯韦特庄园的生活。她一生中从来没有感到如此气恼，如此孤独。另外，她还感到很害怕。

frightened
adj. 害怕的，惊恐的

Language Points to Remember
好句好段记心上

1. It was still raining. Mary was wide awake now.
   外面还在下雨，玛丽现在完全清醒了。
2. The road went up and down, and Mary felt that the journey would never end.
   一会儿上坡，一会儿又下坡，玛丽觉得旅途永远也走不完。

CHAPTER 4
Martha
玛　莎

· QUESTIONS BEFORE READING ·

- Why couldn't Mary dress herself? (Because . ..)
- Who was Dickon?
- What did Mr Craven do with the key of the locked garden?

Mary woke up the next morning when one of the servants came into her room. Outside the window she could see miles and miles of land, that looked like an **endless** red-blue sea. There were no trees.

"What is that?" she asked the servant.

"That's the moor," said the girl, and she smiled kindly. "Do you like it?"

"No," said Mary. "I hate it."

"That's because you don't know it," the servant girl answered. "I love it. It's very beautiful in the spring and summer when the flowers are out. The air smells fresh and the sky is blue and the birds sing."

This servant, whose name was Martha, surprised Mary. She was not like the servants in India, who spoke only when she spoke to them, and who always did what she wanted.

"You are a strange servant," she said.

Martha looked at Mary, who was still in bed, and laughed. She seemed to be a kind person; she had a round, healthy face, and she laughed **a great deal**.

第二天早上，一名女佣进屋时，玛丽醒来了。她看见窗外绵延数英里的土地，看起来像是一片无垠的红蓝相间的大海，没有一棵树木。

endless
adj. 无尽的

“那是什么？”她问那女佣。

“那是草甸子，”那姑娘说，她善意地微笑着，“你喜欢它吗？”

“不，”玛丽说，“我讨厌它。”

“那是因为你还不熟悉它，”那年轻的女佣回答，“我喜欢它。在春夏花开的时候它是很美的。空气很新鲜，天色湛蓝，鸟儿在欢唱。”

这个佣人名叫玛莎，她让玛丽感到惊奇。她不像那些印度的佣人，只有她对他们说话时才说话，而且玛丽要他们做什么，他们就做什么。

“你是个奇怪的佣人。”她说。

玛莎看了一眼仍躺在床上的玛丽，笑出了声。她看起来像是个好人，长着圆圆的脸，面色很健康，很爱笑。

a great deal
adv. 非常

"Are you going to be my servant?" Mary asked.

"I'll help you a bit, but you won't need me much," Martha said.

"Who's going to dress me?" Mary went on.

Martha looked surprised. "Can't you put your clothes on yourself?" she asked.

"No," said Mary crossly. "I've never dressed myself in my life."

"Well," said Martha, "you must learn now."

Mary was very angry now. She did not like this servant who would not help her. And suddenly she felt all alone. She did not understand Martha and Martha did not understand her. Mary started to cry quietly.

Martha felt sorry for the child. She went over to the bed and said kindly: "Eh! You mustn't cry like that. You mustn't. Come, it's time to get up now. I'll help you to get dressed."

Martha's voice was so kind that Mary stopped crying. She got out of bed, and Martha brought her clothes. They were not the clothes which she had had on the journey. They were new.

"Those aren't mine," Mary said. "Mine are black." She looked at the white dress and coat and **added**, "Those are nicer than mine."

"Mr Craven doesn't want you to have black clothes," said Martha.

"I hate black things," said Mary.

While Mary put on her clothes, Martha talked about her family.

“你是要给我当佣人吗？”玛丽问道。

“我会帮你一些忙，可是你不会太需要我。”

“谁给我穿衣服啊？”玛丽继续问道。

玛莎看来很惊讶。“难道你不会自己穿衣服吗？”她问道。

“不会，”玛丽生气地说，“我这辈子没有自己穿过衣服。”

“嗯，”玛莎说，“现在你必须学着穿衣服了。”

玛丽这会儿很生气，她不喜欢这个不肯帮她的佣人。忽然间她感到非常孤单，她不理解玛莎，玛莎也不理解她。玛丽默默地哭了起来。

玛莎可怜这孩子，她走到床边和气地说：“呃，可别那么哭，别哭啦。得了，该起床了。我来帮你穿衣服。”

玛莎语气和善，玛丽不再哭了。她钻出了被窝，玛莎把衣服给她拿来，不是她旅途中穿的那些衣服，是新衣服。

“这不是我的衣服，”玛丽说道，“我的衣服是黑色的。”她看着那白衣裳和外套，又说道：“这些比我的衣服漂亮。”

add
v. 接着说

“克雷文先生不想让你穿黑色的衣服。”玛莎说。

“我讨厌黑色的东西。”玛丽说。

玛丽穿着衣服，玛莎就跟她聊起了自己的家人。

"There are twelve of us," she said. "And my father has very little money. So it's hard for my mother to find enough food. But the children play on the moor, and mother says that the **fresh air** makes them healthy, like the little wild horses which live there. My brother Dickon, who's twelve years old, has a horse."

"Where did he get it?" Mary asked.

"He found it on the moor when it was a baby, and he made friends with it. Now the little horse follows him everywhere, and he **rides** on its back. Dickon is a kind boy, and animals like him."

Mary had always wanted an animal of her own and she began to be interested in Dickon. This was perhaps the first time she had ever been interested in anyone except herself.

Then she and Martha went into the next room, where a meal was waiting. Mary had never been a hungry child, and she did not want to eat now.

"I don't want any food," she said.

"But it's very good," said Martha, who was surprised. "If my brothers and sisters were here, there wouldn't be any food on that table in five minutes time."

"Why?" asked Mary coldly.

"Because they've never had enough food in their lives. They're always hungry."

"I've never been hungry, so I don't know what it's like," Mary said.

"Well," said Martha, "perhaps you ought to try it!"

"Why don't you take the food to your family?" Mary said.

fresh air 新鲜空气

ride *v.* 骑

“我们家有12个孩子，”她说，“我父亲赚钱不多。因此母亲很难让全家人吃饱饭。我们这帮孩子总在草甸子里玩，母亲说新鲜的空气会使他们健康，就像生活在草甸子上的小野马那样。我的弟弟迪康今年12岁，他有一匹马。”

“他从哪儿弄的？”玛丽问道。

“他在草甸子里发现的，那时它还是个小马驹，他和马交上了朋友。他走到哪儿小马就跟到哪，他还骑在马背上。迪康是个好心的男孩子，动物都喜欢他。”

玛丽一直都想有一只自己的动物，她开始对迪康产生了兴趣。这可能是她第一次对自己以外的人感兴趣。

随后她和玛莎到隔壁房间里去了，饭已经准备好了。玛丽从来就没觉得饿，现在也不想吃东西。

“我不要吃东西。”她说。

“可是这顿饭菜多好啊，”玛莎很讶异地说，“要是我的弟弟妹妹们在这里，五分钟之内，这桌上的食物就都吃光了。”

“为什么？”玛丽冷冷地问。

“因为他们这辈子从来没有吃饱过。他们永远饿着肚子。”

“我从来没有饿过，所以我不知道挨饿是什么滋味。”玛丽说道。

“嗯，”玛莎说，“也许你应该尝尝挨饿的滋味！”

“你为什么不把这些吃的拿给家里人？”玛丽说道。

"It's not mine," said Martha **crossly**. "And I can't go home today. I have to work. I can only go home once a month."

At last Mary ate a little food.

"Now go outside and play in the gardens," said Martha. "Perhaps you'll want your food after you've been in the fresh air."

Mary went to the window. It was winter, and it looked very cold outside.

"It's too cold," she said.

"Well, if you don't go outside, you'll have to stay here, and there's nothing for you to do here," Martha answered.

Mary **looked around.** It was true. Perhaps she would go outside and see the gardens.

"Who will go with me?" she asked.

"No one," said Martha. "You must learn to play alone. Dickon goes out on to the moor alone."

When Mary heard about Dickon, she thought that she would go out into the gardens. Martha showed her the way.

"If you go round that way," she said, "you'll come to the gardens." She stopped and then she went on. "One of the gardens is shut up. No one has been inside it for ten years."

"Why?" asked Mary, interested again.

"My Craven shut it ten years ago, when his wife died. He won't let anyone go into it. It was his wife's garden. He shut the door and **hid** the key. But I must go now. Mrs Medlock wants me."

crossly
adv. 乖戾地，不高兴地

“那又不是我的，”玛莎不高兴地说，“再说我今天不能回家。我得干活。我每个月只能回家一次。”

玛丽终于吃了一点食物。

“现在你到花园里玩玩去吧，”玛莎说，“也许呼吸点新鲜空气，你就会想吃东西了。”

玛丽走到窗边，正值冬天，外边看着很冷。

“天太冷了。”她说。

“唉，你要是不到外边去，就只好待在这里，而在这儿你又没有什么事可做。”玛莎答道。

look around
四处张望，环顾四周

玛丽向四周看了看，果真是这样，也许她要出去看看花园。

“谁跟我一起去呢？”她问道。

“谁也不跟你去。”玛莎说道，“你得学会一个人玩。迪康就是一个人到草甸子里去的。”

玛丽听到迪康的名字，于是觉得愿意出门到花园里去。玛莎给她指了路。

“你要是朝那边走，”她说，“就可以走到花园里了。”她停顿了一下，然后继续说道：“有一座花园关着。10 年来从来没有人进去过。”

“为什么？”玛丽又感兴趣了，问道。

“10 年前克雷文先生的妻子故去了，他就把花园关闭了，不许任何人进去，因为那是他妻子的花园。他把门锁上了，还把钥匙藏了起来。我得走了，梅德洛克太太叫我呢。”

hid
v.（hide 的过去式）藏

Language Points to Remember
好句好段记心上

1. Outside the window she could see miles and miles of land, that looked like an endless red-blue sea.
   她看见窗外绵延数英里的土地，看起来像是一片无垠的红蓝相间的大海。
2. Martha's voice was so kind that Mary stopped crying.
   玛莎语气和善，玛丽不再哭了。
3. This was perhaps the first time she had ever been interested in anyone except herself.
   这可能是她第一次对自己以外的人感兴趣。
4. Mary went to the window. It was winter, and it looked very cold outside.
   玛丽走到窗边，正值冬天，外边看着很冷。

CHAPTER 5

Ben Weatherstaff and the Robin

本·韦瑟斯塔夫和知更鸟

· QUESTIONS BEFORE READING ·

- Where was the robin when Mary first saw it?
- How did Ben Weatherstaff call the robin to him?
- When did Mary sound like a "real child"?

After Martha had gone, Mary went into the gardens. She was thinking about the garden that no one had been into for ten years. She wondered what it looked like. She wanted very much to see it. Why had Mr Craven shut it up and **hidden** the key? He had loved his wife, so why did he hate her garden? She wanted to see Mr Craven, but she knew he would not like her.

"People never like me, and I never like people," she thought.

The garden she was in now was certainly not the one which was shut up. She did not think this garden was very pretty, because there was nothing growing in it—only a few trees.

Mary walked through a door into another garden, which was the same as the first one. There was a high wall in front of her at the end of this second garden. She looked for a door in the wall, but she could not find one. She did not think that the gardens ended there, because she could see trees above the wall.

She was still thinking about the secret garden when she saw a little bird with some bright red **feathers** sitting in one of the

玛莎离开以后，玛丽走进了园子。她在想那10年来从未有人进去过的花园。她猜想着它会是什么样子，她非常想看看它。克雷文先生为什么把它锁上并藏起钥匙呢？他爱他的妻子，那么又为什么痛恨她的花园呢？她想见见克雷文先生，但是她知道他不会喜欢自己。

hidden
v.（hide 的过去分词）藏

"人们从来不喜欢我，我也从来不喜欢他们。"她想。

她现在所在的花园当然不是那座被锁的花园。她认为这个花园不怎么漂亮，因为里面没有花草，只有几棵树。

玛丽穿过一道门，进了另一个花园，它和第一座花园一模一样。在玛丽的前方，这个园子的尽头，有一堵高墙。她沿着这堵墙找门，可是没有找到。她认为这不是花园的尽头，因为她还看得见有树木高出墙端。

她正想着那秘密花园的时候，突然看见一只长着鲜亮红羽毛的小鸟栖息在墙那边的一棵树上。忽然

feather
n. 羽毛

trees on the other side of the wall. Suddenly he started to sing—it almost seemed that he was calling to her. His singing made her feel very happy. She was feeling all alone and the little bird made her feel much better. She almost laughed. She liked him.

"Perhaps he lives in the secret garden, and knows all about it," she thought.

She walked back into the first garden and found an old man there. He was working. His face looked cross, and he did not seem to be pleased to see her. But then she did not seem to be pleased to see him.

"What is this place?" she asked him.

"One of the **kitchen** gardens," he answered crossly.

"And what is that?" she asked, and she looked through the door into the second garden.

"Another kitchen garden," he answered, more crossly this time.

"Can I go into the last garden?" she went on.

The old man stopped working. "Which garden?" he asked quickly.

"The one with the high wall," Mary answered quietly. "There were trees on the other side of the wall, and I saw a little bird with red feathers in one of them. He was singing."

To her surprise, the old man suddenly laughed. His face changed, and Mary thought how much nicer a person looks when he laughs.

The old man turned towards the little bird's garden, and began to make a **soft**, kind sound. Then a wonderful thing

间小鸟开始唱歌，简直就好像在召唤她似的。它的歌声使她感到非常高兴。在她感到十分孤单的时候，那小鸟让她感觉好多了。她差一点笑出声来，她喜欢那只小鸟。

“也许它住在秘密花园里，知道那儿的一切。”她想。

她走回第一座园子，发现了一位老人，他正在干活。他满脸愠怒，看见她也并不高兴。话说回来，她看见他也并不见得高兴。

“这是什么地方？”她问他。

kitchen
n. 厨房

“一座菜园子。”他没好气地回答。

“那又是什么地方？”她看着园门外边的第二座园子问道。

“那也是一座菜园子。”他回答道，这回更没有好气了。

“我能进最后那座花园吗？”她追问道。

老人停下了手里的活儿。“哪座花园？”他赶紧问道。

“有高墙的那一座，”玛丽轻声地回答，“墙里边有树，我看见一棵树上有只长着红色羽毛的小鸟。它刚才在唱歌呢。”

令她奇怪的是，老人忽然笑出声来。他的神情变了，玛丽想，人笑起来的样子要好看得多。

soft
adj. 软的；轻柔的；柔和的；温和的

老人转向有小鸟的那座花园，开始发出一种温柔、慈爱的声音。然后发生了一件奇妙的事，那小鸟

happened. The little bird **flew** down and stood on the ground near the old man's foot.

"Where have you been, little one?" the old man asked quietly. He spoke to the little bird as if it were a child. "I haven't seen you at all today."

The little bird put his head on one side and looked at the old man. He was so pretty and he made Mary feel happy.

"Does he always come when you make that sound?" she asked.

"Yes, he does."

"What is he?" she asked.

"Don't you know? He's a **robin**. They're very friendly little birds. He knows that we're talking about him now. He likes to hear people talk about him." And the old man laughed. He seemed to like the little robin very much.

He went on. "When he was a baby, his mother died. He was all alone."

Mary felt strange when she heard this. She went nearer the robin, and said quietly: "I'm all alone, too."

The old man looked at her. "Are you the little girl from India?" he asked.

"Yes," answered Mary.

"Then I'm sure that you're all alone," he said.

"What's your name?" Mary asked him.

"Ben Weatherstaff," he answered, and he laughed. "I'm all alone, too, but not when the robin's with me. He's my only friend."

flew
v.（fly的过去式）飞

robin
n. 知更鸟

飞下来，落在老人的脚边。

“你刚才上哪儿去了，小东西？”老人轻声问道。他和小鸟说话时就像它是一个小孩子那样：“我今天一整天都没见到你啊。”

小鸟歪着头，看着老人。它非常漂亮，玛丽心里很高兴。

“你一发出那种声音，它就会过来吗？”她问道。

“是的，它每次都来。”

“它是什么鸟？”她问道。

“你不知道吗？它是一只知更鸟。知更鸟是友善的小鸟。现在它知道我们在谈论它。它喜欢听别人谈论自己。”老人笑了。他好像很喜爱这只小知更鸟。

他接着说：“它还很小的时候，妈妈就死了。它没有亲人，就它一个。”

玛丽听了这话，有一种奇怪的感觉。她走近知更鸟，轻轻地说：“我也是孤身一人。”

老人看看她。“你就是那个从印度来的小姑娘吗？”他问道。

“是的。”玛丽答道。

“那我肯定你真是孤身一人了。”他说。

“你叫什么名字？”玛丽问他。

“我叫本·韦瑟斯塔夫，”他答道，然后笑了笑，“身边没有知更鸟时，我也是孤身一人。它是我唯一的朋友。”

"I have no friends," said Mary. "I've never had any. I've never played with anyone."

"You and I are the same," Ben went on. "We don't look nice and friendly, and I don't think that we are!"

Mary had never heard the **truth** about herself before. She wondered if she usually looked as cross and unkind as Ben Weatherstaff.

Suddenly the robin began to sing.

"Why is he doing that?" she asked.

"He wants to be your friend," the old man answered.

"My friend?" she asked. "Do you really want to be my friend?" she asked the robin as if she were talking to a person. Her voice was soft and kind, and Ben Weatherstaff was surprised.

"Why," he cried, "you said that very nicely. Perhaps you are a real child and not a cross old woman. You sounded just like Dickon then."

"Do you know Dickon?" Mary asked.

"Of course I do. Everyone knows Dickon Sowerby."

Mary wanted to ask Ben Weatherstaff more questions about Dickon and the robin, but suddenly the robin flew away.

"He has **flown** over the wall," said Mary. "He has flown into the garden which hasn't a door. I want to see that garden so much. There must be a door."

"There was a door ten years ago, but there isn't one now, and that's that," Ben answered, and he sounded cross again. "Now go away. I must work." And quite suddenly, he walked away.

“我没有朋友，”玛丽说道，“我从来也没有过朋友。我从来没有跟别人一起玩过。”

“你和我一样，”本继续说，“我们看来都不友善，而且我觉得我们也的确是这样！”

truth
n. 事实，真相，真理

玛丽以前从来没听到过对自己真实的评价。她纳闷自己是不是经常看来像本·韦瑟斯塔夫那样坏脾气，不友善。

忽然间小知更鸟唱了起来。

“它为什么要唱？”她问道。

“它想做你的朋友。”老人回答道。

“我的朋友？”她问道，“你真的想做我的朋友吗？”她就好像跟人说话似的问那只知更鸟。她的声音又温柔又和气，使本·韦瑟斯塔夫感到很惊奇。

“哈，”他喊道，“你说话很温柔。也许你是一个真正的小女孩，而不是一个坏脾气的老太婆。刚才你听起来正像是迪康。”

“你认得迪康吗？”玛丽问道。

“我当然认得。人人都认得迪康·索尔比。”

玛丽想要再问本·韦瑟斯塔夫一些关于迪康和那只小知更鸟的问题，但是知更鸟突然飞走了。

flown
v.（fly 的过去分词）飞

“它已经飞过墙去了，”玛丽说道，“它飞进那座没有门的花园了。我多想看看那座花园，它肯定有扇门。”

“10 年前有过一扇门，可是现在没有了，就这样。”本回答道，他好像又生气了，“现在你走吧，我得干活了。”他突然转向走开了。

Language Points to Remember
好句好段记心上

1. There was a high wall in front of her at the end of this second garden.
   在玛丽的前方，这个园子的尽头，有一堵高墙。

2. She almost laughed.
   她差一点笑出声来。

3. He likes to hear people talk about him.
   它喜欢听别人谈论自己。

4. Mary had never heard the truth about herself before.
   玛丽以前从来没听到过对自己真实的评价。

CHAPTER 6

The Cry in the Passage

走廊里的哭声

· QUESTIONS BEFORE READING ·

- What made Mary hungry?
- What happened to Mrs Craven in the garden?
- What sound did Mary hear inside the house?

At the beginning of Mary's stay at Misselthwaite Manor, every day was the same. Each morning when she woke up Martha was **lighting** the fire, and a meal was waiting in the next room. Later she went outside into the gardens because there was nothing to do inside the house. Although Mary did not know it, this was the best thing for her.

One morning when she woke up, she felt hungry. At last she knew what it felt like. To her surprise, she ate all her food.

"It's good today," she said to Martha.

"You're hungry because of the fresh air from the moor," Martha said. "Soon you'll be really healthy."

"But I have nothing to play with in the gardens," said Mary.

"Nothing to play with!" cried Martha. "My brothers and sisters play with **whatever** they can find. They just run about and look at things."

And that is what Mary did.

She went to one part of the gardens more than any other: to the place where she had first seen the robin. A lot of

玛丽刚住进米瑟斯韦特庄园时，每天过的都是一模一样的。每天早晨她醒来时，玛莎都是正在给壁炉生火，隔壁房间里早餐已准备好了。稍后她就出去到园子那里，因为在宅子里面无事可做。虽说玛丽自己并不明白，这对于她可是再好不过的事。

light
v. 点火

一天早上，她醒来后觉得肚子饿了。她终于知道了饿是什么滋味。她把早餐吃了个精光，这使她感到吃惊。

"今天早餐很好吃。"她对玛莎说。

"你感到饿，是因为从草甸子上过来的新鲜空气，"玛莎说，"你很快就会真正健壮起来。"

"可是我在园子里没有什么可玩的。"玛丽说。

"没有可玩的！"玛莎喊道，"我的弟弟妹妹们找到什么就玩什么。他们只是四处乱跑，看这看那。"

whatever
pron. 无论什么

而这正是玛丽所做的事。

有一部分园子她最常去：就是她头一次看到知更鸟的地方，墙边生长着茂密的墨绿色植物。有一天她

dark green plants grew there by the wall. One day Mary was wondering why there were so many plants there when suddenly she heard the robin singing. He was sitting on the top of the wall, and he looked down at her, with his little head on one side.

"Oh!" cried Mary. "Is it you—is it you?" She spoke to him as if he were a person who could answer her. And he did answer her—he sang. Mary felt that she knew what he was saying: "Good morning! Isn't the wind nice? Isn't the sun nice? Isn't everything nice? Come on! Come on!"

And Mary began to laugh. "I like you! I like you!" she cried and she tried to sing, too. He flew away suddenly and sat in a tree on the other side of the wall. Mary remembered that the tree was in the secret garden. She wished that she could **fly over** the wall and see the garden.

Mary stayed outside all day, and she thought about the garden a great deal. That evening, when she sat down to eat, she felt hungry and tired, but she did not mind when Martha started to talk. After dinner, she sat in front of the fire, and Martha sat down beside her. At last Mary asked a question which she had wanted to ask for a long time.

"Why does Mr Craven hate the garden?"

"Are you still thinking about that garden?" Martha asked. "I knew you would. I was the same when I first heard about it."

"But why does he hate it?" Mary asked again.

At first Martha did not answer, but then she told Mary everything she knew.

"Now remember this," she began, "Mrs Medlock said that

正在纳闷为什么那里有那么多植物，忽然听到了知更鸟在歌唱。它正栖息在墙头上，俯视着她，小脑袋歪在一边。

“噢！”玛丽喊道，“是你吗——是你吗？”她同它讲话，就好像它是一个能接腔答话的人似的。它真的回答她了——它歌唱了。玛丽感到自己懂得它在说些什么：“早上好！这风不是很柔和吗？这阳光不是很和煦吗？一切不是很美好吗？来吧！来吧！”

玛丽开始笑了。“我喜欢你！我喜欢你！”她喊道，也试着唱歌。它突然飞开，栖息在墙那边的一棵树上。玛丽记起那树长在秘密花园里。她但愿能够飞过墙头，看看那个花园。

fly over
飞越

玛丽整天都待在外面，老是琢磨着那个花园。当天晚上她坐下来进餐时，感到又饿又累，可是玛莎开始聊天时她并不厌烦。晚饭后她坐在炉火前，玛莎也在她身边坐了下来。玛丽终于把很久以前就想问的一个问题说出口来。

“克雷文先生为什么痛恨那花园呢？”

“你还在惦记那花园吗？”玛莎问道，“我知道你会想它的。我头一次听到这件事的时候也是一样。”

“可是他为什么恨它呢？”玛丽又问。

玛莎起初没有回答，后来她把所知道的一切都告诉了玛丽。

“你要记住，”她开始说，“梅德洛克太太说过我

we mustn't talk about it; so don't tell anyone that I told you."

Mary said that she would not tell, so Martha went on: "It was Mrs Craven's garden. She made it when they were first married, and she loved it very much. She and Mr Craven took care of it themselves, and the **gardeners** never went into it. There was a tree in the garden where Mrs Craven used to sit. One day part of the tree broke and she fell. She was very badly hurt, and the next day she died. Mr Craven was so sad that the doctors thought he would die too, but he didn't. He has been sad **ever since**, poor man. There—now you know why he hates the garden and never goes into it."

Mary did not ask any more questions. She felt very sorry for Mr Craven. Outside on the moor the wind was making a noise, and Mary was glad that she was inside the house. Suddenly, she heard another noise. It sounded almost the same as the wind, but it was inside the house. It sounded like a child crying far away.

"Can you hear someone crying?" she said.

"No," Martha answered quickly. "It's only the wind."

Then the crying came again, and somewhere in the house a door closed.

"There!" said Mary. "Someone is crying. I told you so! And it's a child."

This time Martha answered crossly. "It was the wind or one of the servants who has had a **headache** all day."

们不许谈论花园的事，所以千万不要告诉别人是我跟你说的。”

玛丽说她不会告诉别人，于是玛莎就接着说："那是克雷文夫人的花园。他们刚结婚时她开辟了这座花园，她非常喜欢它。她和克雷文先生亲自料理花园，园丁们从来不进去。花园里有一棵树，克雷文夫人常坐在树上。有一天树枝断了，夫人跌了下来。她伤得很重，第二天就死了。克雷文先生伤心极了，医生们都以为他也会死的，可是他没有死。他从那时起一直很忧伤，可怜的人。就是这样——现在你知道他为什么痛恨那座花园，为什么从来不进去了。”

gardener
n. 园丁

ever since
自从

玛丽没再问问题，她很为克雷文先生难过。外面的草甸子上风在呼呼作响，玛丽很庆幸她是在宅子里面。突然，她听见另外一种声音，听起来几乎和风声一样，可是它来自宅子里面。听起来好像是个孩子在远处哭泣。

“你听得见有人在哭吗?”玛丽说。

“没有，”玛莎马上回答，“只是风声。”

那哭声又传过来了，宅子里不知何处传来关门的声音。

“听！”玛丽说道，“是有人在哭。我告诉过你！还是个孩子在哭。”

这一回玛莎没好气地回答：“是风的声音，要不就是那个头痛了一整天的佣人。”

headache
n. 头痛

Language Points to Remember

好句好段记心上

1. Although Mary did not know it, this was the best thing for her.

   虽说玛丽自己并不明白，这对于她可是再好不过的事。

2. She wished that she could fly over the wall and see the garden.

   她但愿能够飞过墙头，看看那个花园。

3. Outside on the moor the wind was making a noise, and Mary was glad that she was inside the house.

   外面的草甸子上风在呼呼作响，玛丽很庆幸她是在宅子里面。

CHAPTER 7
"There was someone crying—there was!"

"刚才有人在哭——真的!"

· Questions before Reading ·

- How many rooms were there in the house?
- What did Mrs Medlock do to Mary?

The next day it was raining, and Mary could not see the moor outside the window.

"What am I going to do today?" she asked Martha. "I can't go out into the gardens and there is nothing to do here."

"Can you read?" Martha asked.

"Yes," answered Mary.

"Well, why don't you read?" Martha said.

"I haven't any books," Mary answered.

"Perhaps Mrs Medlock will let you go into the room where Mr Craven keeps his books," Martha went on.

But Mary did not ask where this room was. She wanted to find it by herself. And so, after Martha had gone, she opened the door of her room, and went into the **passage** to look for Mr Craven's books. She did not really **mind** whether she found the room or not, but Mrs Medlock had told her about the hundred rooms during the train journey, and Mary wanted to see inside some of them.

Mary walked a long way that morning. There were many passages in the house, and many, many doors. She felt very

第二天下雨了，玛丽从窗子望出去看不见草甸子。

“我今天干什么呢？”她问玛莎，“我既不能到园子里去，这儿又无事可做。”

“你识字吗？”玛莎问道。

“我识字。”玛丽答道。

“那好，你为什么不看书呢？”玛莎说。

“可我没有书。”玛丽回答说。

“也许梅德洛克太太会让你进克雷文先生的书房。”玛莎接着说。

可是玛丽没有问这间房子在哪里，她想要自己找到它。所以，玛莎走了以后，她就开了房门到走廊里去找克雷文先生的书。她并不真正在乎能不能找到那间屋子，但是来的时候，在火车上梅德洛克太太跟她谈起过关于100 间房间的事。玛丽想找几间屋子看看里面是什么样子的。

passage
n. 过道，走廊
mind
v. 介意

那天上午玛丽走了很多路。宅子里有许多走廊，还有许许多多的门。她走过这些房门时心里有种异

strange as she walked past them. At last, on the second floor, she opened one of the doors. Inside was a big bedroom. After that, she opened more and more doors, until she began to think that she had been into every room in the house.

She lost her way two or three times when she tried to find her own room again. At last she reached her own floor, but she still could not find her own room.

"How quiet it is!" she thought.

Just then, however, she heard a sound—the same sound that she had heard the night before.

"It's nearer than it was last night," she thought.

Suddenly a door opened, and there was Mrs Medlock. She was very angry when she saw Mary.

"What are you doing here?" she shouted. "Didn't I tell you to stay in your own room?"

"I made a mistake," Mary answered. "I thought I heard someone crying." She really hated Mrs Medlock now.

"Of course you didn't hear anyone crying," Mrs Med lock said. "Go back to your room at once, or I'll hit you hard." And she **pulled** Mary along the passage to her room.

"Now stay there," she said. "Mr Craven was right. You need a teacher. I've no time to take care of a child."

When she had gone, Mary sat down in front of the fire. She did not cry, but she was very angry and sad at the same time.

"There was someone crying—there was—there was!"

样的感觉。终于，在三楼，她打开了其中的一扇门，里面是一间很大的卧室。此后，她打开了越来越多的房门，直到她感觉自己已经进过宅子里每一个房间了。

她想回自己的房间，却有两三次走迷了路。终于她回到了自己的楼层，可是还是找不到自己的房间。

“多么安静呀！”她想道。

然而就在这时候，她听到了一个声音，和头一天晚上听到的一模一样。

“这次比昨晚更近一些了。”她想。

忽然间一扇房门开了，梅德洛克太太站在那儿。她看见玛丽时怒气冲天。

“你在这里干什么？”她吼道，“我不是告诉过你，叫你待在自己的屋里吗？”

“我错了，”玛丽回答道，“我好像听见有人在哭。”她现在真的恨上梅德洛克太太了。

“你绝对没听见有人在哭，”梅德洛克太太说，“你马上回到自己的房间里去，不然我就要狠狠地揍你。”说着她拉着玛丽沿着走廊回到玛丽自己的房间。

pull
v. 拉，拽

“现在待在这里，”她说，“克雷文先生没错，你需要一位老师。我没有时间照料孩子。”

她走了以后，玛丽在炉火前坐了下来。她没有哭，但是她非常气愤，同时也非常悲伤。

“刚才的确是有人在哭——是有人在哭——是有人在哭！”

Language Points to Remember
好句好段记心上

1. She did not really mind whether she found the room or not, but Mrs Medlock had told her about the hundred rooms during the train journey, and Mary wanted to see inside some of them.
   她并不真正在乎能不能找到那间屋子，但是来的时候，在火车上梅德洛克太太跟她谈起过关于100 间房间的事。玛丽想找几间屋子看看里面是什么样子的。

2. At last she reached her own floor, but she still could not find her own room.
   终于她回到了自己的楼层，可是还是找不到自己的房间。

CHAPTER 8

The Key of the Garden

花园的钥匙

· QUESTIONS BEFORE READING ·

- What was the nice fresh smell?
- What did Mary see near the robin?
- Why did she keep it?

Two days later, when Mary woke up in the morning, she sat up in bed and called to Martha: "Look, the sun is shining!"

"Yes," said Martha. "Spring is coming."

"I thought it always rained in England," said Mary.

"Oh no, of course it doesn't," laughed Martha. "Yorkshire's the **sunniest** place on earth sometimes."

"I'd like to see your house very much," said Mary.

"I'll ask my mother," said Martha. "I don't have to work today, so I'm going home."

"I like your mother," Mary said, "although I've never met her. And I like Dickon, too, although I've never met him."

"I wonder what Dickon would think of you?" Martha said.

"He wouldn't like me," said Mary. "No one ever does."

Martha looked **thoughtful**, and then she said: "But do you like yourself, Mary?"

Mary thought, and then she answered: "Well . . . no, not really—but I've never thought of that before."

Martha laughed. "Mother said that to me once, when I was

两天以后，玛丽早上醒来，从床上坐了起来，向玛莎叫道："快看，太阳出来了！"

"不错，"玛莎说，"春天来了。"

"我还以为英格兰总是下雨呢。"玛丽说。

"不是，当然不是，"玛莎笑道。"有时候约克郡是世界上阳光最明媚的地方。"

sunniest
adj.（sunny 的最高级）阳光明媚的

"我很想看看你们家的房子。"玛丽说。

"我去问问我母亲，"玛莎说，"我今天不用干活，所以我要回家去。"

"我喜欢你的母亲，"玛丽说，"尽管我从来没有见过她。我也喜欢迪康，尽管我也从来没有见过他。"

"我不知道迪康会怎么看你。"玛莎说。

"他不会喜欢我的，"玛丽说道，"从来没有人喜欢过我。"

thoughtful
adj. 思考的

玛莎看起来若有所思，然后她说道："可是，你喜欢你自己吗，玛丽？"

玛丽想了想，然后回答："嗯……不喜欢，并不真正喜欢，不过我以前没有想过这个。"

玛莎笑了："我母亲有一次就是这么跟我说的，

saying unkind things about people. It made me laugh so much that I stopped being unkind and cross."

Later Martha went home to see her family. Mary felt very alone. She went out into the gardens and ran and ran. Then she began to feel better. The sunshine made everywhere look nicer. She went into the first kitchen garden and she found Ben Weatherstaff there. Ben seemed to be happier because of the sunshine, too. For the first time he spoke to her before she spoke to him.

"Spring's coming. Can you smell it?" he asked.

Mary thought she could. "I can smell something nice and fresh," she said.

"That's the spring in the earth," Ben said. "It's making things grow. Soon you'll see the little green **points** coming up out of the earth."

Soon she heard the robin. He, too, was very happy this morning. He walked about near Mary's feet.

"Do you remember me?" she asked him.

"Remember you!" cried Ben Weatherstaff almost crossly. "Of course he remembers you! He knows everything in this garden. He's never seen a little girl before, and he Wants to know more about you."

"Are things growing in his garden?" Mary asked.

"What garden?" Ben asked angrily.

"The one where he lives. Are the flowers there dead?" Mary wanted to know so much.

"Ask him," said Ben, and he looked down at the robin. "He's

当时我正在说别人的坏话。她的话让我大笑了一回，之后就不再对别人刻薄、发脾气了。”

后来玛莎回家去看望家人了，玛丽感到非常孤单。她出去到园子里跑了又跑，然后才开始感觉舒畅一些。阳光下到处都更好看了。她走进第一个菜园子，看到本·韦瑟斯塔夫在那里。因为阳光普照，本看起来也高兴多了。他头一回主动同玛丽说话。

“春天来了。你闻到它的气息了吗？”他问道。

玛丽觉得自己闻到了。“我闻到一种清香、新鲜的气味。”她说。

“那是泥土里春的气息。”本说道，“是它使万物生长。很快你就会看到尖尖的小绿芽从土里钻出来。”

point
n. 尖

不久她就听见知更鸟的叫声，它今天早上也很开心，它在玛丽脚边走来走去。

“你还记得我吗？”她问它。

“记得！”本·韦瑟斯塔夫几乎是生气地喊道，“它当然记得你！这园子里的事儿它都知道。它以前从来没有见到过小姑娘，它想多多了解你。”

“那个花园里也长东西吗？”玛丽问道。

“什么花园？”本生气地问道。

“它住的花园。那里面的花都死了吗？”玛丽非常想知道。

“你问它吧，”本说道，向下看着知更鸟，“只有

the only one who knows."

Ten years was a long time, Mary thought. She was born ten years ago. She thought that she liked the secret garden in the same way that she liked the robin and Dickon and Martha's mother. She went to walk by the wall where she had first seen the robin. And then — the most wonderful thing happened—all because of Ben Weatherstaff's robin.

He was standing near her on the earth by the wall. He had followed her. She was so pleased that she cried out. "You *do* remember me! You do! How wonderful!"

Then suddenly she saw something in the earth near the robin: it was a metal **ring**. She **bent down** to look at it. And it was not just a ring—there was a key, too. It looked very old.

Mary stood and looked at the key. "Perhaps it's the key to the secret garden," she thought. She stood there for a long time. If it really was the key to the secret garden, she would be able to go there whenever she liked—if she could find the door. Then nobody would know where she was. She liked this thought very much.

She walked up and down by the wall. It seemed so foolish, she thought, to be so near the garden, to have the key, and not to know where the door was. But she kept the key so that she would be ready if she found the door.

它才知道。"

玛丽想10年的时间可不短。她自己是10年前出生的。她觉得自己喜欢那秘密花园，就像自己喜欢这知更鸟，喜欢迪康和玛莎的母亲一样。她沿着第一次见到知更鸟的墙边散步，然后，最奇妙的事发生了，这都是因为本·韦瑟斯塔夫的知更鸟。

它挨着墙，站在她脚边，它是跟着她走过来的。她高兴得叫了起来;"你真的记得我！真的！多好呀！"

然后她突然看见知更鸟近旁的土里有一样东西：那是个金属环。她弯下腰去看了看，这不仅是一枚金属环，上面还有一把钥匙，看上去很古旧。

ring
n. 环，圈
bent down
（bent 为 bend 的过去式）弯下身，弯腰

玛丽站在那儿，看着那把钥匙。"也许这是秘密花园的钥匙。"她站在那里想了很久。如果这真的是秘密花园的钥匙，那她想什么时候进去就能什么时候进去，如果她能找到园门的话。那时谁都不知道她在哪里，她很喜欢这个想法。

她沿着墙根走来走去。她想，离花园这么近，又有了钥匙，却不知道门在哪里，这是多么愚蠢的事。于是她收起了钥匙，这样找到了门就可以用上了。

Language Points to Remember
好句好段记心上

1. Martha looked thoughtful, and then she said: "But do you like yourself, Mary?"
   玛莎看起来若有所思，然后她说道："可是，你喜欢你自己吗，玛丽？"

2. She went out into the gardens and ran and ran.
   她出去到园子里跑了又跑。

3. She went to walk by the wall where she had first seen the robin.
   她沿着第一次见到知更鸟的墙边散步。

CHAPTER 9

The Secret Garden

秘密花园

· QUESTIONS BEFORE READING ·

- Why hadn't Mary seen the door before? (Because plants . . .)
- What work did Mary do in the garden?
- What did Mary and Martha write?

The next morning Martha was back. She told Mary all about her day at home.

Then Mary went outside and into the part of the gardens where she had found the key. Then she saw the robin, and she laughed because she knew that he had followed her.

"You showed me the key yesterday," she said to him. "Perhaps you'll show me the door today, but I don't believe that you know where it is!"

When she was in India, she had heard a great deal about **magic**, and she always said that what happened next was magic. She was standing near the wall when suddenly the wind blew the plants to one side. She looked—and there in the wall was a door. Her heart beat noisily. She could not believe it! She found the key hole in the door and the key went in quite easily. She tried to turn it—it was difficult, but it did turn.

She looked behind her quickly, but there was no one near. Then she took a deep breath, opened the door, and went inside quickly. She shut the door behind her.

She could not believe it! She was standing inside the secret

第二天早上玛莎回来了。她把前一天家里的情况都告诉了玛丽。

然后玛丽出门，进了花园，来到她发现钥匙的地方。这时她看见了那知更鸟，她笑了，因为她知道那鸟儿是在跟着她走。

“你昨天让我找到了钥匙。”她对鸟儿说，“也许你今天会让我找到门，可是我不相信你知道门在哪里！”

她在印度的时候，听到过不少关于魔法的事，所以她总说接下来发生的事就是魔法。她站在墙边时，突然一阵风把植物都吹到一边。她看了看，果然在墙上有一扇门。她的心跳得砰砰响。难以置信！她找到门上的钥匙孔，一下子就把钥匙插进去了。她试着转动钥匙，这挺费劲，可是终于还是转动了。

magic
n. 魔法

她迅速向身后看了一眼，旁边没有人。然后她深深地吸了一口气，打开门，快步跨进去，随手把门关上。

她真不敢相信！她已经站在秘密花园里了！

garden!

The garden was the strangest place Mary had ever seen. It was like a garden in a **fairy** story. There were high walls all around, and because it was winter, all the plants were brown and dead-looking. There was no green anywhere, and Mary did not know whether the garden was **alive** or dead. After ten years the trees had grown so much that they had made bridges over the **spaces** between each other.

"How quiet it is!" said Mary softly. Even the robin, who was sitting at the top of his tree, did not move. "And I am the first person who has spoken here for ten years!"

She walked around the garden with the robin, who wanted to show her everything. It was so quiet that she felt that she was a hundred miles away from anyone, and yet she did not feel alone. She had found a world of her own. As she walked around the garden, she noticed a lot of little green points which showed above the earth.

"They must be spring flowers," she thought. "The garden isn't quite dead." This made her feel happy.

Mary did not know anything about gardening, but the grass grew too closely around the little green points, so she pulled it up to give the flowers more space to grow. And this was how she passed her first morning in the secret garden. She was very busy. When it was time to go into the house to eat she could not believe that she had been working for three hours.

"I'll come back this afternoon," she said happily.

At lunch she ate so much that Martha was pleased. They

fairy
adj. 神话的，神仙的

alive
adj. 活着的；存在的；活跃的

space
n. 空间

这花园是玛丽见到过的最怪异的地方，它像是童话故事里的花园。四周都是高墙，而且因为是在冬天，草木都是棕色的，像枯死了一样。到处看不见一点绿意，玛丽不知道花园是否还有生机。这10年来树木疯长，在树木之间的空地上方，枝桠交错搭成了桥。

"多么安静呀！"玛丽轻声说道。连那只知更鸟也一动不动，它正栖息在属于它的那棵树梢上。"我是10年来第一个在这里说话的人！"

她和知更鸟一起在园里四处走着，那鸟儿好像要她把整个花园看个遍。四周非常安静，她感到自己好像与其他所有人相隔遥远，可是她并不觉得孤单。她已经发现了自己的天地。她在花园里到处走着，发现地上许多小绿芽儿冒出了头。

"这些一定是春天的花，"她想道，"这花园并没有完全死去。"这让她感到高兴。

关于园艺的事，玛丽一点儿也不懂，可是草长得离那些绿芽儿太近了。她就把草拔掉，好给花儿更多的地方生长。她在秘密花园里的第一个上午就这样度过了。她一直忙碌着，到了该回宅子里去吃饭的时候，她简直不能相信自己已经干了三个小时了。

"我今天下午还要来。"她欢喜地说。

午饭时她吃得非常多，玛莎感到很高兴。她们

talked about plants and flowers during the meal, and Mary asked Martha questions about the things she had seen that morning. She was careful not to say which part of the garden she had been in.

After lunch Mary sat by the fire and said quietly: "I wish I had a little **spade**."

Martha laughed. "What do you want a spade for? Are you going to use it in the garden?"

"Yes, Martha. I'd like to make a little garden of my own. I'd like to plant **seeds** and watch flowers grow."

"Well!" said Martha. "My mother was right. She said that you should have a little garden of your own. She thought that it would make you happy."

"Your mother knows a lot of things, doesn't she?" said Mary. "I wonder how much a little spade costs?"

"Not much," Martha answered.

"I've got quite a lot of money," Mary said.

"I wonder . . ." said Martha thoughtfully. "Yes, I know. We'll write to Dickon and ask him to buy you a spade and some seeds."

"But how will I get the things when Dickon buys them?"

"He'll bring them himself," said Martha.

"I will see him at last!" cried Mary. "I want to see him so much."

So together Martha and Mary wrote Dickon a letter.

边吃边谈着树木和花草，玛丽问了玛莎许多问题，都是关于她上午看到的东西。她小心翼翼地避免谈到自己去的是园子里的哪一部分。

午饭后玛丽坐在炉火旁，轻声地说："我真想有一把小铲子。"

spade
n. 铲子

玛莎笑了："你要一把铲子做什么？你想用它在花园里干活吗？"

"是的，玛莎。我想给自己弄个小花园。我想要撒点种子，看着花儿生长。"

seed
n. 种子

"喔！"玛莎说道，"我母亲说的对。她说你应该有个自己的小花园。她觉得它会让你开心的。"

"你母亲懂得很多，不是吗？"玛丽说，"我不知道买一把小铲子要多少钱？"

"要不了多少钱。"玛莎回答说。

"我有不少钱。"玛丽说。

"我不知道……"玛莎思忖着说，"对，我知道了。我们给迪康写一封信，让他给你买一把铲子和一些种子。"

"可是迪康买来以后，我怎么才能拿到呢？"

"他会自己带来的。"玛莎说。

"我终于能见到他了！"玛丽大声说道，"我特别想见到他。"

于是玛莎和玛丽一起给迪康写了一封信。

Language Points to Remember
好句好段记心上

1. She was standing near the wall when suddenly the wind blew the plants to one side.
   她站在墙边时，突然一阵风把植物都吹到一边。

2. After ten years the trees had grown so much that they had made bridges over the spaces between each other.
   这10年来树木疯长，在树木之间的空地上方，枝桠交错搭成了桥。

3. She was careful not to say which part of the garden she had been in.
   她小心翼翼地避免谈到自己去的是园子里的哪一部分。

CHAPTER 10

Dickon

迪　康

· QUESTIONS BEFORE READING ·

- What did Dickon bring?
- What secret did Dickon keep all the time?

The sun **shone** every day for the next week, and Mary often went to her secret garden. It was like a fairy garden, and she loved it. She liked being outside in the wind; she liked working around the little green points. It really was a secret garden—because no one knew where she was. She liked this thought most.

During that week, she and Ben Weatherstaff talked a great deal more. He almost seemed to like her now, and although he often sounded cross, she began to like him, too. He told her more about the plants and flowers that she had found in the secret garden. But again she was very careful not to tell him too much.

One day at the end of the week, Mary was playing near some trees in one of the kitchen gardens when she heard a strange, low sound. She wanted to know what it was, so she went nearer. And then she saw Dickon. As soon as she saw the boy, she knew that he must be Dickon.

He was standing under a tree, and all around him were little animals. He was playing a **pipe** very softly. None of the

shone
v.（shine 的过去式）照耀

接下来的一周，每天都阳光明媚，玛丽也常常到她的秘密花园里去。它就像是个仙园，她很爱它。她喜欢到户外吹吹风，她喜欢在地里的绿尖芽边干活。这真是个秘密花园，因为没有人知道她在哪里，一想到这儿她就很开心。

这一周里，她和本·韦瑟斯塔夫谈了很多。现在他看来似乎喜欢她了，虽然他时常听起来像是很生气，她也开始喜欢上了他。他更详细地向她介绍了她在秘密花园里见到的花木。可是她同样很小心，避免告诉他太多。

周末的一天，玛丽正在菜园子里的树丛旁玩耍，忽然听见一种奇怪的、低低的声音。她想知道这是什么声音，所以就走近了一些，这时她看见了迪康。她一看见那男孩，就知道他一定是迪康。

pipe
n. 笛子

他正站在一棵树下，身旁围着许多小动物，他正轻柔地吹奏一根笛子。甚至在玛丽向他走过去时，

animals looked frightened even when Mary came towards him.

"I'm Dickon," he said, "and I know you are Mary."

He was about twelve years old, his nose turned up at the end, and he had very blue eyes. He had a wide mouth and he laughed a great deal. He was not a good-looking boy, but he was very friendly. He spoke to Mary as if he knew her well, and as if he liked her, too.

"I've brought your spade and your seeds," he said.

Mary had not met many boys in her life, and she did not quite know what to say to Dickon. At last she said: "Will you show me the seeds, please? Let's sit down and look at them."

"Well," said Dickon. "These are little white flowers which smell lovely. Then these are a beautiful **deep** red colour." Then he stopped and listened. "Where's that little robin who's singing to us?"

"He's in that tree," said Mary. "He's Ben Weatherstaff's robin, but he knows me, too."

"Yes, he does," said Dickon. "And he likes you."

"Do you understand everything that birds say?" Mary asked him. She could not believe that she was really talking to Dickon at last.

"Well," said Dickon. "I think I do, and they think I do. And that's what's important."

Dickon laughed, and then he talked a lot more about the seeds. He told her how to plant them. Suddenly he turned to her and said: "Tell me where your garden is. We can go and plant the seeds together."

小动物们也没露出害怕的样子。

“我是迪康。”他说道，“我知道你是玛丽。”

他大约有12岁，鼻尖翘翘的，眼睛湛蓝。他嘴巴很宽，总爱笑。他长得并不好看，但是很友善。他和玛丽说话时就好像跟她很熟似的，也好像他很喜欢她。

“我把你要的铲子和种子带来了。”他说。

玛丽长这么大还没有见过几个男孩子，因此她不大清楚该对迪康说什么。她终于说道：“能给我看一下花种子吗？我们坐下来看看吧。”

“好，”迪康说，“这些种出来的是小白花，很香。那些是美丽的深红色的花。”然后他停了下来，聆听了一会儿：“给我们唱歌的那只小知更鸟在哪儿？”

deep
adj. 深色的

“它在那棵树上，”玛丽说道，“那是本·韦瑟斯塔夫的知更鸟，可是它也认得我。”

“对，它认得你，”迪康说，“而且它喜欢你。”

“鸟儿们说的话你都听得懂吗？”玛丽问他。她简直不敢相信她终于是在和迪康谈话了。

“噢，”迪康说，“我想我是都懂的，而且它们也觉得我懂，这才是重要的。”

迪康笑了，然后他又介绍这些花种，他告诉她怎样把种子种下去。忽然他向她转过身来，说道：“告诉我你的花园在哪里。我们可以去一起播种。”

Mary's face went red and then white and then red again. She did not know what to say. Dickon could not understand why she did not answer. At last she said. "Can you keep a secret?"

Dickon still did not understand, but he said. "Of course I can. I **keep secrets** all the time. I don't tell other boys where the animals and birds live, do I?"

"Listen," said Mary very quickly. "I've **stolen** a garden. No one owns it, and no one wants it. No one takes care of it—only me. I shall die if anyone takes it from me."

Dickon was surprised because Mary loved the garden so much. "Where is it?" he said quietly.

"Come with me, and I'll show you," she answered, and she led him into her secret garden.

"This is my secret garden," she said, when she had shut the door behind them, "and I am the only person in the whole world who wants it to be alive."

玛丽的脸红了，然后又转白，又变红了。她不知道该说什么，迪康无法理解她为什么不回答。最后她说："你能保守秘密吗？"

迪康仍然不明白，可是他说道："我当然能，我无时不刻都在保守秘密。我没告诉别的男孩子小动物和小鸟们住在哪里，是不是？"

"听着，"玛丽飞快地说，"我偷来了一个花园。它没有主人，谁都不要它。没有人打理它，只有我一个人。要是有人把它从我这儿夺走，我会死的。"

迪康听到玛丽这么爱那花园，感到很惊讶。"它在哪儿？"他小声问道。

"跟我来，我指给你看。"她回答，接着把他领到她的秘密花园里去了。

"这就是我的秘密花园，"她把园门在身后关好，说道，"而且我是世界上唯一想要它充满生机的人。"

keep secret
保守秘密

stolen
v.（steal 的过去分词）偷

Language Points to Remember
好句好段记心上

1. She liked being outside in the wind; she liked working around the little green points.
   她喜欢到户外吹吹风，她喜欢在地里的绿尖芽边干活。

2. He spoke to Mary as if he knew her well, and as if he liked her.
   他和玛丽说话时就好像跟她很熟似的，也好像他很喜欢她。

3. Dickon was surprised because Mary loved the garden so much.
   迪康听到玛丽这么爱那花园，感到很惊讶。

CHAPTER 11

Dickon Sees the Secret Garden

迪康见到了秘密花园

· QUESTIONS BEFORE READING ·

- Dickon already knew about the secret garden. Who had told him?
- Mary now liked five people. Who were they?

Dickon stood and looked round and round the garden.

"Eh!" he said very softly. "It's a strange place. But it's very pretty. It's as if it were asleep."

Then he walked all round the garden **as** quietly and **softly as** Mary had done on her first morning there.

"I never thought that I'd see this place," he said at last.

"Did you know about it'?" asked Mary.

"Ssssh! Speak quietly," said Dickon. "Someone might hear us. Yes, I knew about it. Martha told me."

"Will there be roses in the summer?" Mary asked. "Are the plants alive or dead? Can you tell?"

"They aren't all dead," said Dickon. And he took his knife and **cut** a piece **off** one of the rose trees. Although it looked dead on the outside there was a little green part inside. It was still alive. "There's a lot of dead wood here," he went on. "We ought to cut it away. But the tree is alive for sure."

"Oh, I'm so glad it's alive," said Mary. "Let's go round the garden to see which plants are still alive."

And together they went from tree to tree and plant to

迪康站在那里，对花园四处看了又看。

“呃！”他轻轻地说，“这是个奇怪的地方，但是它非常美丽，它就好像睡着了。”

as . . . as . . .
和……一样
softly
adv. 柔和地，轻声地，静静地，轻轻地

然后他轻手轻脚地在花园里到处走了走，就像玛丽第一个早上进来时那样。

“我从来没想到我会看到这个地方。”他又说道。

“你过去听说过这个花园吗？”玛丽问。

“嘘！小点声。”迪康说，“可能会有人听见。是的，我听说过，玛莎告诉我的。”

“夏天会有玫瑰花吗？”玛丽问道，“这些植物是死是活，你看得出来吗？”

cut off
切断，中断，使死亡

“并不是全死了，”迪康说，他拿出小刀，从一株玫瑰树上割下一小段树枝。尽管从外面看是已经死了，可是里面有一点绿色的部分，它还活着。“这里有不少树枝已经死了，”他接着说，“我们应当把它们砍掉。可是树肯定还活着。”

“噢，我真高兴它还活着。”玛丽说，“咱们在园里到处走走，看看哪些还活着。”

然后他们俩一起从一棵树走到另一棵树，从一

plant. Then Dickon showed Mary how to use the spade. They both worked very hard that morning. Suddenly Dickon noticed some of the places where Mary had moved the grass from around the little green points.

"Who did that?" he asked.

"I did," answered Mary.

"I thought you didn't know anything about gardening," he said.

"I don't," she said.

"Well, you did the right thing, Mary. You've done a lot of work, haven't you?"

"Yes," said Mary. "And it's making me strong. I don't feel tired any more, and I love the smell of the **earth**."

Then Dickon said, "But there's still a lot more work to do here."

"Will you help me to do it?" Mary asked him. "Please, Dickon, please."

"Of course I'll help you." he answered. "I'll come every day if you want me to. I want to make this garden alive again more than anything in the world. We'll have a lot of fun together."

He began to walk about thoughtfully. Then he said: "But I don't want this garden to look like the other big gardens. I don't want it to be too **orderly**, do you?"

"No," said Mary. "I don't. I like it the way it is now. If we make it too orderly, like other gardens, it won't be a secret any more." She stopped and thought, and then she said: "Dickon, you're as nice as Martha said you were. I like you very much. I

棵植物走到另一棵植物。接着，迪康示范给玛丽看怎样使用铁铲。那天上午他们俩都干得很起劲。忽然间迪康注意到在一些小绿芽周围玛丽已经把野草除掉了。

“这是谁做的？”他问道。

“是我。”玛丽回答。

“我本来以为你对于栽花种草一无所知呢。”他说。

“我确实不懂。”她说。

“嗯，你做得很对，玛丽。你在这儿已经干了不少活，是不是？”

“是的，”玛丽说，“它使我身体强壮起来了。我现在不再感到疲倦了，而且我喜欢泥土的味道。”

earth
n. 土壤，泥土

迪康说：“可是这儿还有很多的活要干。”

“你肯帮我干吗？”玛丽问他，“求求你了，迪康。”

“我当然要帮忙了，”他答道，“要是你愿意，我天天来。我要让这所花园重新生机盎然，这是我在这个世界上最大的愿望。我们在一起会很开心的。”

他开始若有所思地走来走去，接着又说：“可是我不想让这座花园看起来和别的大花园一样。我不想让它太整齐划一，你看呢？”

orderly
adj. 整齐地

“对，”玛丽说，“我也不想那样。我喜欢它现在的样子。我们要是把它打理得太整齐划一，像别的花园一样，它就不再是个秘密了。”她停下来想了想，又说道：“迪康，你正像玛莎所说的那么善良。我很

like five people now."

Dickon laughed. "Only five people?" he asked. "Who are the other four?"

"Your mother and Martha, and the robin and Ben Weatherstaff." Then she asked thoughtfully: "Do you like me?"

"Yes, I do," he answered. "And so does the robin. We both like you very much."

Then they worked again. Mary felt so happy; she remembered that first morning with Dickon for the **rest** of her life. It was time to go back to the house to eat too soon, and she had to leave Dickon. He had his food with him, so he stayed in the garden. Mary did not want to leave him. She was frightened that he might go away and never come back.

When she left, she said: "You will never tell anyone, will your?"

"Eh! No, Mary, I won't tell anyone. You're as safe in this garden as the animals and the birds are on the moor." And Dickon laughed. Mary knew that he was telling the truth.

喜欢你。我现在喜欢五个人了。”

迪康笑了。“只喜欢五个人吗？”他问道，“还有四个是谁呢？”

“你母亲和玛莎，知更鸟和本·韦瑟斯塔夫。”然后她满怀心事地问，“你喜欢我吗？”

“是的，我喜欢你，”他答道，“知更鸟也喜欢你。我们俩都很喜欢你。”

rest
n. 剩余

接着他们又开始干活。玛丽感到高兴极了，她一辈子记得和迪康在一起度过的第一个上午。该回宅子去吃饭了，时间过得太快，她得离开迪康了。他随身带着午饭，所以就待在花园里。玛丽不愿离开他，她害怕他会走开，永远不再回来。

她离开时，说：“你永远不会告诉别人，是不是？”

“呃！玛丽，不会的，我谁都不告诉。你在这花园里会像小鸟和动物在草甸子上一样安全。”迪康笑了。玛丽知道他说的是真心话。

Language Points to Remember
好句好段记心上

1. Then he walked all round the garden **as** quietly and **softly as** Mary had done on her first morning there.
   然后他轻手轻脚地在花园里到处走了走，就像玛丽第一个早上进来时那样。

2. I want to make this garden alive again more than anything in the world.
   我要让这所花园重新生机盎然，这是我在这个世界上最大的愿望。

3. She was frightened that he might go away and never come back.
   她害怕他会走开，永远不再回来。

CHAPTER 12

Mary Meets Mr Craven

玛丽见到克雷文先生

· Questions before Reading ·

- What did Mary ask Mr Craven for?
- What was his answer?

"I've seen Dickon!" Mary cried as soon as she saw Martha. "I've seen him!"

"And do you like him?" asked Martha.

"I think that he's . . . wonderful!" said Mary.

She ate her meal quickly because she wanted to go back to Dickon, but Martha stopped her.

"Mary," she said. "Mr Craven has come back. He wants to see you."

Mary's face went white for the second time that day. "But why?" she asked. "He didn't want to see me when I first came to Misselthwaite. Why does he want to see me now?"

"Don't be frightened," said Martha. "He's going away again tomorrow, and he won't come back until next winter."

Then Mrs Medlock came in. She took Mary to see Mr Craven. Mary was very frightened. She knew that her uncle was not going to like her, and that she was not going to like him.

He was sitting in an **armchair** by the fire.

"Come here!" he said to her.

Mary went towards him, and she became the ugly, cross

玛丽一看见玛莎就喊道："我看见迪康了。我看见他了！"

"你喜欢他吗？"玛莎问她。

"我觉得他……棒极了！"玛丽说。

她飞快吃完了午饭，因为她想回到迪康身边去，可是玛莎拦住了她。

"玛丽，"她说，"克雷文先生回来了。他想见见你。"

在那一天玛丽的脸色第二次发白了。"可是为什么呀？"她问道，"我刚来米瑟斯韦特时他不想见我。现在他为什么要见我？"

"别害怕，"玛莎说，"他明天又要走了，要到冬天才回来。"

接着，梅德洛克太太进来了，她带着玛丽去见克雷文先生。玛丽很害怕，她知道她的舅舅不会喜欢她，而且她也不会喜欢舅舅。

armchair
n. 扶手椅

他坐在壁炉边的扶手椅上。

"过来！"他对她说。

玛丽走到他面前，她又变成那个从印度来的坏

little girl from India. She looked at her uncle carefully. He was not really a hunchback, although he did not sit very **straight**. His face was very sad.

"Are you well?" he asked her.

"Yes," she answered.

"Do they take good care of you?"

"Yes."

"You are very **thin**," he went on.

"But I'm getting fatter," Mary answered. She wanted to say more, but she could not.

Then he asked her, "Are you happy? Do you want a teacher? Do you want anything?"

"Oh, please, I don't want a teacher yet," said Mary. "But there is one thing I'd like . . . May I . . . may I have a little piece of earth?"

"Earth?" her uncle said, surprised. "What do you mean?"

"To plant seeds in—to watch things grow—to make a garden," Mary answered. She was very frightened that he was going to say no.

Mr Craven looked very strange when she said this. He seemed to remember something. "A piece of earth," he said quietly. "Yes, of course you can have a piece of earth. Take as much as you want, and make it come alive." He looked very tired now, and said. "You must go now. I am very tired. I'm going away tomorrow. I won't be back until next winter."

As Mary walked back to her room, she thought: "He is

straight
adv. 笔直的，挺直的

thin
adj. 瘦弱的，薄的

脾气的丑丫头了。她仔细地看着她的舅舅。他并不真的是个驼背，虽说他坐得不十分挺直。他的面容很哀伤。

“你身体好吗？”他问她。

“好。”她答道。

“他们照料的你周到吗？”

“周到。”

“你很瘦。”他接着说。

“可是我开始长肉了。”玛丽回答。她想多说几句话，可是说不出来。

然后他问她，“你在这儿快乐吗？你想要一位老师吗？你缺什么吗？”

“噢，求你了，我还不想有老师。”玛丽说，“可是有一样东西是我想要的……我可不可以……可不可以有一小块地？”

“地？”她的舅舅感到惊讶地说，“你是什么意思呢？”

“好撒下种子，看它们长起来，弄一个花园。”玛丽说，她很怕他会不同意。

她说这些话时，克雷文先生表情很奇怪，他好像回忆起什么事。“一块地，”他轻声地说，“是的，你当然可以有一块地。你想要多大就要多大，把它打理活。”这时他看来很疲倦，他说道：“你现在得走了。我很累了。我明天要走了，要到冬天才回来。”

玛丽走回自己的房间时，心里想：“他真是个好

really a nice man, but he looks so sad. Poor, Mr Craven."

When she got back to her own room, it was **too** late **to** go to the secret garden again that day. But she hoped that Dickon would come back the next day.

人，可是看起来多么悲伤。可怜的克雷文先生。”

那天她回到自己房间时已经很晚，不能再回到秘密花园去了，但是她希望迪康第二天会回来。

too . . . to . . .
太……不能干

Language Points to Remember

好句好段记心上

1. Mary's face went white for the second time that day.

   在那一天玛丽的脸色第二次发白了。

2. He was not really a hunchback, although he did not sit very straight.

   他并不真的是个驼背，虽说他坐得不十分挺直。

3. When she got back to her own room, it was too late to go to the secret garden again that day.

   那天她回到自己房间时已经很晚，不能再回到秘密花园去了。

CHAPTER 13
"I Am Colin"
"我是科林"

· Questions before Reading ·

- What was Colin's full name?
- Why didn't Colin's father want to see him?
- How did Mary send Colin to sleep?

During the night, however, it began to rain. Mary woke up and could not go to sleep again because she felt too cross. The wind was making a crying noise around the house, and the sound of it made her feel sad.

Then suddenly the noise changed. "It isn't the wind now," she said. "It's the crying that I heard before."

She got out of bed, took a **candle** and went out into the passage. She went to the place where she had seen Mrs Medlock on the day that she had opened doors. The noise was nearer. Someone was crying. She listened at the door. Yes, someone was crying in that room.

She opened the door quickly. Inside there was a bedroom with a large bed in it. A boy was lying on the bed, and he was crying. He did not seem to be **in pain**, but he sounded tired and cross. He was about ten years old, and he had a thin, white face. His eyes were very big and he did not look very healthy.

"Who are you?" the boy asked. He was frightened. "Are you real?"

"Of course I'm real," Mary answered. She was frightened,

夜里下起了雨。玛丽醒了，再也无法入睡，因为她感到很不开心。风在宅子四周刮得呜呜作响，好像在哀泣，这声音使她感到忧伤。

然后那声音忽然变了。"现在不是风声了，"她说，"这是我以前听到过的哭泣声。"

candle
n. 蜡烛

她下了床，拿上一支蜡烛来到了走廊里。她走到那天开门看见梅德洛克太太的地方。那声音近了，有人在哭泣。她在门口听了一会儿，不错，有人在那间屋里哭呢。

她迅速打开门，里面是一间卧室，有一张大床。床上躺着一个男孩，他在哭。他不像是身上哪儿疼，可是他听来好像很疲倦，很不高兴。他大约有10岁，脸色苍白，面容很瘦。他的眼睛特别大，看起来身体不太好。

in pain
在疼痛中

"你是谁呀？"男孩问道，他很害怕："你是真人吗？"

"我当然是真的。"玛丽回答。她也很害怕，"你

too. "Are you real?"

He looked at her hard. "Yes, I am. I'm Colin Craven. Who are you?"

Mary looked at him hard, too. "I'm Mary Lennox. Mr Craven is my uncle. I came to live here when my mother and father died."

"Mr Craven is my father," said the boy.

"No one told me that my uncle had a son," Mary said.

"Come here," the boy said. "You are real, aren't you? I often see people when I'm asleep. You might be one of them," and he **touched** her hand.

"Did no one tell you that I was here?" she said.

"No," he answered. "Because they thought it might make me ill. I don't want people to see me. I don't want people to talk about me."

"Why not?" asked Mary.

"Because I'm always ill. I'm going to be a hunchback if I live. But I **shan't** live."

"This is a very strange house," Mary said quietly. "Everything is a secret. Does your father come to see you?"

"Not often," answered Colin. "He doesn't want to see me. When he sees me, he thinks about my mother. She died when I was born. I think he hates me."

"He hates the garden because she died," Mary said thoughtfully.

"What garden?" the boy asked.

"Oh—just a garden that she used to like—that's all. Mr Craven shut the garden when his wife died, and he hid the key.

是真人吗？”

他盯着她：“是的，我是。我是科林·克雷文。你又是谁呢？”

玛丽也盯着他：“我是玛丽·伦诺克斯。克雷文先生是我的舅舅。父母去世后，我就来这里住了。”

“克雷文先生是我父亲。”男孩说。

“没有人告诉我说我舅舅有个儿子。”玛丽说。

“过来，”男孩说，“你是真人，不是吗？我睡着的时候常看见人。你可能就是其中之一。”说着，他碰了碰她的手。

touch
v. 触摸；感动；接触

“没有人告诉你我来了吗？”她说。

“没有，”他回答，“因为他们认为那可能会使我生病。我不想让别人看见我，也不想让别人议论我。”

“为什么呢？”玛丽问道。

“因为我总是生病。我要是不死，会成为驼背人，可是我会死掉的。”

shan't = shall not

“这真是一所很奇怪的宅子，”玛丽轻声说道，“无论什么事都是秘密。你爸爸常来看你吗？”

“他不常来，”科林回答道，“他不想见到我，他一见到我就想起我母亲，她是在生我的时候死的。我想他痛恨我。”

“他因为她死了，就恨那花园。”玛丽若有所思地说。

“什么花园？”男孩问道。

“噢，只是她过去喜欢的一所花园，没有别的。克雷文先生在妻子死后把花园关了，还把钥匙藏了起

No one has been into the garden for ten years."

But Colin wanted to know more about the garden. He asked her to tell him about it. Where was it? Had she looked for the door? Had she asked the gardeners about it? When Mary told him that no one would talk about it, he said something which frightened her very much.

"I could make them talk about it," he said. "All the servants must do what I want. If I live, Misselthwaite Manor will be mine one day, and they know that."

Mary was sad because Colin did not seem to want to live. But at that minute, she was more frightened that he would tell everyone about the secret garden.

"I want the servants to find the key, and to open the door," he went on. "I want them to take me there in my **wheelchair**." For the first time in his life Colin was interested in something.

"Oh, please . . . don't . . . don't do that!" Mary cried.

"Why not?" he asked. He did not understand. "I thought you wanted to see it."

"I do," she answered, "but if you make them open the door, it will never be a secret again."

But Colin still did not understand. "A secret?" he asked. "What do you mean?"

So Mary tried to tell him. "You see," she said, "if we can find the garden, it will be our own garden. Only we will know about it. Don't you see? It will be much more fun if it's a secret."

At last Colin began to understand. "I've never had a secret

来。10 年来没人进去过。”

可是科林想多听听关于花园的事，他请求她给他讲讲。花园在哪里？她有没有找过那扇门？有没有问过园丁们花园的事？玛丽告诉他谁也不肯谈那座花园，他说了一句话，把她吓得不轻。

“我可以强迫他们谈那座花园，”他说，“所有的仆人都必须照我的意思做。我如果活着，有朝一日米瑟斯韦特庄园就是我的，他们都知道这一点。”

玛丽感到悲伤，因为科林好像不想活下去。不过此时，她更害怕科林会把秘密花园的事告诉大家。

“我要叫仆人们找到那钥匙，打开那扇门，”他接着说，“我要叫他们用轮椅把我推到那里去。”科林有生以来第一次对一件事情感兴趣了。

wheelchair
n. 轮椅

“噢，求求你，不要……不要那样做！”玛丽喊。

“为什么不要？”他不能理解，“我还以为你想要看它呢。”

“我是想看，”她答道，“可是如果你强迫他们打开门，花园就不再是个秘密了。”

可是科林还是不明白：“秘密？你是什么意思？”

玛丽试着给他解释。“你要明白，”她说道，“假如我们能找到那所花园，它将是我们自己的花园。只有我们自己知道它。难道你不明白吗？如果它是个秘密，那会好玩得多。”

科林终于开始明白了。“我从来没有什么秘密，

before, but I think that secrets are nice."

Mary went on, "Perhaps we can find a boy to **push** your wheelchair, and then we can go to the garden alone. No one will know where we are. Then it will always be a secret garden. And you can come outside in the wind and the **sunshine**, and you will get better."

Then she said, "Will Mrs Medlock be very angry if she finds me here?"

"She will do what I tell her to do," said Colin. "I'm glad that you came tonight, and that's the only thing that's important."

"And I'm glad I came," said Mary.

"But I want you to be a secret, too," said Colin. "I shan't tell them about you. I'll only tell Martha. She will tell you when I want to see you. She often takes care of me."

"So Martha knew about you all the time?" Mary asked. Now she understood why Martha had looked so frightened when she had heard Colin before.

They talked for a long time. At last Mary said, "I've been with you a long time. You must sleep now. I'll sing to you and then perhaps you'll go to sleep. My servant in India used to sing this song to me."

Mary began to sing very softly. Soon Colin went to sleep, and Mary went back to her own room.

push
v. 推

sunshine
n. 日光，日照

可是我想有秘密会很不错的。”

玛丽接着又说：“也许我们能找到一个男孩子给你推轮椅，然后我们可以单独到那去。没有人会知道我们在哪里，那样花园将永远会是秘密花园，而且你还可以到外面去晒晒太阳，吹吹风。你的病就会好的。”

她又说：“要是梅德洛克太太发现我在这里，她会不会很生气？”

“她会照我的要求做，”科林说，“我很高兴你今天晚上来了，这才是唯一重要的事情。”

“我也很高兴我来了。”玛丽说。

“可是我想要连你也成为一个秘密，”科林说，“我不告诉他们关于你的事，我只告诉玛莎一个人，我想见你时她会告诉你。她常常来照料我。”

“那么说，玛莎一直都知道你的事？”玛丽问道。现在她明白了以前她听见科林在哭时，玛莎为什么显得那么害怕。

他们俩谈了很久，最后玛丽说道：“我在你这里很长时间了，你得睡觉了。我给你唱歌，也许你就能睡着了，在印度时我的佣人常给我唱这首歌。”

玛丽开始轻轻地唱了起来。科林很快就睡着了，玛丽又回到自己的房间去了。

Language Points to Remember
好句好段记心上

1. She got out of bed, took a candle and went out into the passage.

   她下了床，拿上一支蜡烛来到了走廊里。

2. He doesn't want to see me. When he sees me, he thinks about my mother.

   他不想见到我，他一见到我就想起我母亲。

3. But at that minute, she was more frightened that he would tell everyone about the secret garden.

   不过此时，她更害怕科林会把秘密花园的事告诉大家。

4. Now she understood why Martha had looked so frightened when she had heard Colin before.

   现在她明白了以前她听见科林在哭时，玛莎为什么显得那么害怕。

CHAPTER 14
Martha Is Frightened
玛莎吓坏了

· QUESTIONS BEFORE READING ·

- What did the doctor from London say about Colin?
- How did Colin speak to Martha? (Like . . .)
- What will Dr Craven get if Colin dies?

It was still raining next morning. Mary could not go outside. When Martha came in, Mary told her. "I know who was crying."

A look of great fear went across Martha's face.

"Oh no!" she cried. "How?"

"I heard the noise again in the night," said Mary. "And I went to see what it was. It was Colin. I found him."

"Oh Mary," said Martha. "What have you done? I didn't tell you anything, but now they'll **send** me **away**. What shall I do?"

"They won't send you away, Martha," said Mary. "He liked me. We talked for a long time. He was glad that I came."

"Was he?" asked Martha. "Are you sure?" She did not **believe** Mary. "Did he let you look at him?"

"Yes. I looked at him all the time," Mary answered. "I think he liked me."

"I can't believe it. It must be magic," Martha said quietly.

"He wants me to talk to him every day," Mary went on. "He's not going to tell Mrs Medlock. It's a secret. He'll tell you when he wants to see me. Then you can tell me." She stopped. "What's

第二天早上，天还在下雨，玛丽不能出去了。玛莎进来时，玛丽告诉她说：“我知道是谁在哭了。”

玛莎的脸上掠过非常恐惧的表情。

“噢，不！”她喊道，“你是怎么知道的？”

“我夜里又听见那声音了，”玛丽说道，“我就走过去看看是怎么回事。是科林，我找到他了。”

“唉，玛丽，你都干了些什么呀？我什么也没有告诉你，可是现在他们要赶我走了。我怎么办呢？”

send away 送走，把……打发走

“他们不会赶你走的，玛莎。”玛丽说，“科林喜欢我，我们聊了很长时间，他很高兴我来了。”

“真的？”玛莎问，“你能肯定吗？”她不相信玛丽的话，“他让你看他的样子了吗？”

believe v. 相信

“是的，我一直看着他。”玛丽说，“我觉得他喜欢我。”

“真是难以置信，一定是有魔法。”玛莎轻声地说道。

“他想要我每天和他聊天，”玛丽接着说，“他不会告诉梅德洛克太太，这是个秘密。他什么时候想见我，就会告诉你，那样你就能转告我。”她住口不说

wrong with him?" she asked.

"No one really knows," said Martha. "After his wife's death Mr Craven didn't want to see the baby. He thought that the child was going to be a hunchback. He almost wanted the child to die."

"But Colin isn't a hunchback," said Mary. "He didn't look like one."

"No, he isn't yet," said Martha. "But his father is frightened because his back is weak. Colin knows this. An important doctor came from London once. He saw Colin, and said that he wasn't a hunchback, and he wasn't going to be one. He said that the boy must go out in the fresh air. But Colin didn't believe him."

"I wonder," said Mary. "I got better when I went outside and watched flowers and plants growing. Do you think that Colin would get better, too?"

"I don't know. He says that he hates the garden and the wind. He had his worst illness when they took him into the rose garden. He thinks that he's going to die. He only sits in bed and reads books."

That afternoon Martha told Mary that Colin wanted to see her.

"It's magic," she said. "He has got up out of bed, and he's sitting in an armchair."

Mary went quickly. She did not want to see Colin as much as she wanted to see Dickon, but she wanted to see him very much.

In **daylight** Colin's room was very beautiful. It was warm and **pleasant**.

了。“他得的什么病？”她问道。

“谁也不清楚，”玛莎说，“克雷文先生在他的妻子死后，不想看见他的孩子，他认为孩子会是个驼背。他几乎希望孩子会死掉。”

“但是科林并不驼背，”玛丽说，“他看起来不像个驼背。”

“不像，他到现在还不是，”玛莎说，“可是他的父亲很害怕，因为他的背不结实。科林知道这件事，有一回他们从伦敦请来一位名医。他给科林看了病，说科林不是驼背，也不会变成驼背。他说那孩子必须出去呼吸点新鲜空气。可是科林不相信他。”

“我有些相信，”玛丽说，“自从我出去看花木生长那时候起，身体就比以前好了。你是不是认为这样科林的身体也会变好呢？”

“我不知道，他说他讨厌花园和风。他闹病最重的那一回，就是因为他被带到玫瑰园里去，他觉得自己会死。现在他只是坐在床上看书。”

当天下午玛莎告诉玛丽说科林想见她。

“这真是魔力，”她说，“他下床了，坐在扶手椅里呢。”

玛丽立即去了，虽然不如想见迪康那么迫切，但她还是非常想看见科林。

在白天，科林的房间很美，温暖而舒适。

daylight
n. 白天，日光
pleasant
adj. 舒服的

"Come in," said Colin. "I've been thinking about you all morning."

"I've been thinking about you, too," said Mary. "Poor Martha, she's very frightened. She thinks that they will send her away. But she didn't tell me about you. I found you by myself."

"Tell Martha to come here," Colin said.

When Martha came in, he said: "You have to do what I want, don't you?"

"Yes, Colin," Martha answered.

"You are not to be frightened that they will send you away. If you do what I want, I will take care of you. That is all."

Martha went out. She looked very surprised. Mary looked thoughtful.

"What are you thinking about?" Colin asked her.

"I'm thinking about two things. Firstly, that you are like an Indian **prince** that I once saw. He spoke to his people **in the same way** that you speak to Martha. Everybody had to do what he wanted. He wasn't very nice."

"And what was the second thing?" Colin asked.

"I was thinking about you and Dickon. You are not at all like him."

"Who is Dickon?" he asked.

Mary wanted to talk about Dickon. "He's Martha's brother. He's twelve years old, and there is no one in the world like him. He can talk to every animal and bird. He plays a pipe very softly and they come to listen. He has lived on the moor all his life, and he knows where all the animals and birds live."

"进来吧。"科林说道，"我整个上午都在想着你。"

"我也在想着你。"玛丽说，"可怜的玛莎，她很害怕。她以为他们会把她赶走。可是她并没有对我提过你，是我自己找到你的。"

"你去叫玛莎到这儿来。"科林说。

玛莎进来后，科林说："我让你做什么事，你都得做，对吗？"

"是的，科林。"玛莎答道。

"你不用害怕他们会把你赶走。你如果照我说的做，我会照顾你。就这样吧。"

玛莎出去了，她显得非常惊讶。玛丽看上去好像在想心事。

"你在想些什么？"科林问道。

"我在想两件事。第一件事是，你像我见过的一个印度王子。他对臣民说话的方式同你和玛莎说话时一样，人人都得按他的要求去做。他可不怎么讨人喜欢。"

prince
n. 王子
in the same way
以同样的方式

"第二件事呢？"科林问道。

"我在想你和迪康，你一点也不像他。"

"迪康是谁呀？"科林问道。

玛丽愿意谈迪康的事。"他是玛莎的弟弟。他今年12岁，与众不同。他能和每种动物和小鸟谈话，他只要轻轻地吹起笛子，动物和鸟儿们就来聆听。他一辈子都是在荒草甸子上度过的，他知道动物和小鸟们都住在什么地方。"

"I never see anything because I'm ill," said Colin sadly. "I can't go on the moor."

"Why not?" asked Mary. "You might go one day."

"No, I won't. I'm going to die. Everyone wants me to die."

"Don't be foolish. Who wants you to die?" Mary asked.

"The servants and Dr Craven. He's my father's brother. If I die, he'll get Misselthwaite Manor. I think that my father wants me to die, too."

"Oh no, he doesn't," said Mary. This talk of death made her feel sad. "Don't let's talk about death," she said. "Let's talk about life. Let's talk about Dickon."

They talked about Dickon and his mother and their little house on the moor. They talked about the little green points in the garden, and about Ben Weatherstaff's robin. They laughed about everything, and Colin felt happy. He did not remember that his back was weak.

Suddenly, Dr Craven and Mrs Medlock walked into the room. Dr Craven looked very frightened when he saw Mary.

"What's this?" he cried. "Are you all right, Colin? Are you all right?"

"Of course I'm all right," said Colin, and he spoke like the Indian prince again. "This is Mary Lennox. I asked her to come. I like her. I want to see her often. No one told her about me," he went on, because Mrs Medlock looked cross and frightened **at the same time**. "She heard me one night when I was crying, and she found me by herself."

Dr Craven told Colin he must remember that he was ill.

“我什么都没见过，因为我有病。”科林伤心地说，“我不能到草甸子里去。”

“为什么不能？”玛丽问，“也许有一天你就能去。”

“不，我不能。我是要死的，人人都想要我死。”

“别傻了。谁会想让你死呀？”玛丽问。

“仆人们和克雷文医生。他是我父亲的兄弟，我要是死了，他就会得到米瑟斯韦特庄园。我想连我父亲也想要我死。”

“噢，不，他不想。”玛丽说。谈论死亡令她感到哀伤。“咱们别谈论死亡了，”她说道，“咱们谈生活吧，咱们谈谈迪康吧。”

他们就谈论迪康、他的母亲和他们家在草甸子上的小房子。他们谈到花园里嫩绿的幼芽，还谈到本·韦瑟斯塔夫的知更鸟。他们不管谈到什么事都笑，科林感到很快乐，他忘记了他的脊背不结实。

忽然间，克雷文医生和梅德洛克太太走进屋里来了。克雷文医生看见玛丽时，显得很惊慌。

“这是怎么回事？”他喊道，“你没事吧，科林？你没事吧？”

“我当然没事了。”科林说道，他说话又像那位印度王子了。“这是玛丽·伦诺克斯，我请她进来的，我喜欢她，我要常常见她。谁也没对她提起我的事。”他接着说，因为梅德洛克太太的样子显得又是惊惧又是生气，“有一天夜里我哭的时候，她自己找到了我。”

at the same time 同时

克雷文医生告诉科林说他必须记住他有病，然

Then he and Mrs Medlock went away.

"But I don't want to remember that I'm ill," Colin said to Mary as soon as they had gone. "I don't remember when I'm with you. That is why I like you, Mary. Now we'll have tea together and you can tell me more about India."

During the next week, Mary saw Colin every day. The week went very quickly, and the two children had a great deal of fun together. There was only one thing which Mary had to remember. She wanted to tell Colin that she had been inside the secret garden, but she did not know whether he could keep the secret. By the end of the week, however, Mary was sure that Colin would get better if he went outside. She knew that he did not want anyone to see him, but at last she asked him. "Would you be angry if Dickon saw you?"

"No, I don't think so," he answered. "Dickon is the one person in the world who wouldn't make me angry."

后他和梅德洛克太太走了。

“可是我不想老记得我有病。”他们一走，科林就对玛丽说，“我和你在一起时就忘了我有病，我喜欢你就是为此。现在我们要一起喝茶，你可以多跟我讲讲印度。”

之后的一周内，玛丽每天都去看科林。一个星期很快地过去了，这两个孩子在一起玩得很尽兴。只是，玛丽得记住一件事情。她想告诉科林她已经到那秘密花园里去过，可是她不知道科林能不能保守这个秘密。但到了周末，玛丽已经确信科林如果到外面去，身体就会好一些。她知道他不愿意让别人看到他，可最后还是问他说：“如果让迪康看到你，你会生气吗？”

“不，我想不会。”他答道，“迪康是全世界唯一不会惹我生气的人。”

Language Points to Remember
好句好段记心上

1. A look of great fear went across Martha's face.
   玛莎的脸上掠过非常恐惧的表情。
2. In daylight Colin's room was very beautiful. It was warm and pleasant.
   在白天，科林的房间很美，温暖而舒适。
3. He spoke to his people in the same way that you speak to Martha. Everybody had to do what he wanted.
   他对臣民说话的方式同你和玛莎说话时一样，人人都得按他的要求去做。
4. They talked about the little green points in the garden, and about Ben Weatherstaff's robin.
   他们谈到花园里嫩绿的幼芽，还谈到本·韦瑟斯塔夫的知更鸟。
5. By the end of the week, however, Mary was sure that Colin would get better if he went outside.
   但到了周末，玛丽已经确信科林如果到外面去，身体就会好一些。

CHAPTER 15
The Secret Garden Again
重返秘密花园

· QUESTIONS BEFORE READING ·

- What was the robin doing?
- What did people believe about Colin's back?

The next day Mary woke up very early, After a week of rain, the sky was blue again, and the sun was shining.

"It's warm," cried Mary. "The garden will begin to grow again. Oh, how wonderful!" She got out of bed and opened the window. "I must see the secret garden now!" she cried. "I can't wait!"

She **dressed** quickly and ran out into the gardens.

"I'm sure that Dickon will come today," she thought, and she ran even faster towards the secret garden.

But Dickon was in the garden before her. She saw him when she opened the door. He was working hard, and some of his animals were with him.

"Dickon!" Mary cried. "How did you get here so early? The sun has only just got up!"

Dickon laughed. "Eh!" he said, "I got up before the sun did. I couldn't stay in bed."

"Oh Dickon," Mary said. "I'm so happy."

They looked at all the new plants together. The green points had become flowers at last, and the roses were alive.

第二天，玛丽早早就醒了。下了一星期的雨，天空又转为蔚蓝，阳光灿烂。

“真暖和，”玛丽大声说道，“花园里的花草又要长起来了。噢，多么美妙啊！”她下了床，打开窗子。“我现在必须去看看秘密花园！我等不及了！”她喊道。

她很快穿好衣服，跑到外面园子里。

dress
v. 穿衣，给……穿衣

“我敢打赌迪康今天会来。”她想道，就加快脚步跑向秘密花园。

可是迪康已经比她早到花园了。她一打开园门就看见了他。他正在卖力地干活，他的一些小动物们也和他在一起。

“迪康！”玛丽喊道，“你怎么这么早就到了这里？太阳才刚升起来。”

迪康笑了。“呃！”他说，“我起得比太阳早，我在床上待不住。”

“噢，迪康，”玛丽说，“我真高兴。”

他们俩一起看着那些新长出来的花株。那些绿色的小芽儿终于变成花朵了，玫瑰复苏了。到了夏天，

Later in the summer there would be flowers on them. Even the plants which **grew** on the walls were be coming green.

"Everything is alive again," Mary said.

Suddenly Dickon stood quite still. He had seen the robin's red feathers. The little bird had just flown into a big tree.

"Keep still," Dickon told Mary. "He's working hard. He has found a wife and he's making a home for her where she can **lay** her eggs. We mustn't frighten him while he's **building** it. If we do, he'll never be our friend again."

So Mary and Dickon sat on the grass. Dickon spoke to Mary very softly. He told her not to watch the robin because that would frighten him.

"We mustn't talk about him, then," said Mary, "or I will watch him. There is something I want to ask you, Dickon. Do you know about Colin?"

Dickon turned to her and said, "Why? What do you know about him?"

"I've seen him," she answered. "He likes me. He says that when he is with me he doesn't remember that he's going to die."

"Well," said Dickon. "I'm glad that you know about him. I knew about him, but I had to hide it from you. I don't like hiding things."

"How do you know about Colin?" Mary asked him.

"Everyone knows that Mr Craven has a son," he answered. "But no one ever sees him, because he's a hunchback. Mr Craven can't look at the boy because he's so like his mother.

它们将开满繁花。连攀在墙上的植物都透出了绿意。

grew
v.（grow 的过去式）生长

“花草树木又充满生机了。”玛丽说。

忽然间迪康站住不动了，他看见了知更鸟鲜红的羽毛。那小鸟儿刚飞上一棵大树。

“别动，”迪康对玛丽说，“它在努力干活。它找到了妻子，正为她搭窝，供她生蛋。它筑巢时，我们不要吓着它。如果吓着了它，它就永远不会再和我们做朋友了。”

lay
v. 下蛋
build
v. 建造

于是玛丽和迪康在草地上坐了下来。迪康很轻声地和玛丽说着话，他叫她不要看着知更鸟，因为那样会吓着它。

“那么我们就不要谈论它了，”玛丽说道，“不然我就会看它的。迪康，我有一件事要问你。你知道科林的事吗？”

迪康朝她转过脸来，说道：“为什么这么问？你对他了解多少？”

“我见到他了。”她回答说，“他喜欢我。他说他和我在一起时就会忘了他是要死的人。”

“嗯，”迪康说道，“我很高兴你知道他的事了。我早就知道他的，可是我不得不瞒着你。我可不喜欢对人瞒着事儿。”

“你怎么知道科林的事？”玛丽问迪康。

“大家都知道克雷文先生有个儿子，”他答道，“可是谁也没有见过他，因为他是个驼背。克雷文先生不敢看那男孩，因为他太像他的母亲了。可怜的克雷文

Poor Mr Craven, he wishes that the child had never been born."

"He isn't a hunchback," said Mary. "But he thinks that he's going to be one. It's very sad. I've been thinking, Dickon," she went on. "Do you think that Colin could keep our secret?"

"I think so," said Dickon. "If he could, we could bring him out into the garden in his wheelchair. I'm sure that he would get better in the fresh air."

"The doctor from London said that he would," said Mary.

"Well, we must bring him out here **as soon as possible**," said Dickon.

Mary and Dickon worked very hard that morning. Mary went into the house for a meal, but she went out to the garden again quickly.

"Tell Colin that I can't come yet," she said to Martha. "I'm very busy in the garden. Dickon is waiting for me."

"Colin will be cross," answered Martha, but Mary did not listen.

先生，他但愿那孩子没出生过。”

“他并不是驼背，”玛丽说，“可是他以为他会长成一个驼背，这事真惨。迪康，我一直在想，”她接着说，“你说科林能保守我们的秘密吗？”

“我觉得他能，”迪康说，“如果他能，我们可以让他坐在轮椅上，把他带到花园里。我肯定他呼吸些新鲜空气，病会好的。”

“从伦敦来的那位医生说他会的。”玛丽说道。

“好吧，我们得把他带到这里来，越快越好。”迪康说。

as soon as possible 尽可能快地

玛丽和迪康当天上午干活很卖力。玛丽进屋去吃饭，可是她很快又出来，到了花园里。

“告诉科林我去不了他那儿了，”她对玛莎说，“花园里有很多活要干，迪康在等我。”

“科林会生气的。”玛莎回答道，可是玛丽根本不听。

Language Points to Remember

好句好段记心上

1. He was working hard, and some of his animals were with him.
   他正在卖力地干活，他的一些小动物们也和他在一起。
2. If we do, he'll never be our friend again.
   如果吓着了它，它就永远不会再和我们做朋友了。
3. I'm sure that he would get better in the fresh air.
   我肯定他呼吸些新鲜空气，病会好的。

CHAPTER 16
Mary and Colin Quarrel
玛丽和科林吵架了

· QUESTIONS BEFORE READING ·

- Why did Colin and Mary quarrel?
- What did Mary tell Colin about his back?

Mary did not go back to the house until the evening. Then she wanted to tell Colin about Dickon and his animals. But when she saw Martha, she knew that something was not right.

"Colin is very angry because you didn't go to see him," Martha told her.

Mary began to feel cross. The secret garden and Dickon were the two most important things in her life. Colin was fun sometimes, but he was not as important as the garden or Dickon.

She went to see him, however. He was in bed this time.

"Why didn't you come?" he asked her. He spoke like the Indian prince.

"Because I was working in the garden with Dickon," she answered.

Colin looked cross. "I won't let that boy come here again," he said angrily.

This made Mary very cross. "If you send Dickon away, I'll never come into this room again," she **shouted**.

"You'll have to come if I want you to," **cried** Colin.

"I won't," she answered.

玛丽直到晚上才回到宅子里，然后就想告诉科林关于迪康和他的小动物的事。可是她一看见玛莎，就知道出事了。

“科林非常生气，因为你没有去看他。”玛莎告诉她。

玛丽也开始不高兴了，秘密花园和迪康是她生活中最重要的两件事。科林有时候也很有意思，可是他没有那花园和迪康重要。

然而，她还是去看他了，这一回他躺在床上。

“你为什么没有来？”他像那位印度王子一样问玛丽。

“因为我在花园里和迪康一起干活。”她答道。

科林看来是发脾气了。“我不许那孩子再到这里来！”他怒气冲冲地说。

这惹得玛丽很生气。“你要是把迪康赶走，我就永远不再踏进这屋里一步。”她喊道。

“我要你来，你就得来！”科林喊道。

“我就不来！”玛丽答道。

shout
v. 呼喊，呼叫
cry
v. 叫喊

"Yes, you will," shouted Colin.

"No, I won't," Mary shouted.

And they shouted at each other for some time. They said some very unkind things. At last Colin shouted: "Get out of this room!"

And Mary answered: "I'm going, and I won't come back! I wanted to tell you about Dickon and his animals, but I won't now."

She ran out of the room. She felt very angry, but also rather sad. Now she would never tell Colin her great secret.

When she got back to her room, she found some books on the table. They were **presents** from Mr Craven. There were some picture books, and two books about **gardening**.

"How kind he is," she thought, and then she began to think about Colin. She began to feel a little bit sorry for him. "Poor Colin," she thought. "Perhaps he has been thinking about his hunchback all afternoon. Perhaps I will go and see him tomorrow."

She went to bed early because she was tired, but she woke up suddenly during the night. There was a great noise. People were running along the passages, and far away someone was crying.

"It's Colin," she thought. "I don't know what to do, but someone must stop him."

Suddenly Martha came into her room. "Oh, Mary," she cried. "Please stop him! He'll hurt himself. Please stop him! He likes you."

So Mary went to Colin's room. When she saw him, she shouted: "Stop it! Stop it! Stop it! If you cry again, I'll cry too,

“你就得来！”科林高声喊道。

“不，我就不来！”玛丽也高声喊道。

他们俩这样互相嚷嚷了好一会儿，各自都说了些很伤感情的话。科林终于大喊道：“你滚出房间去！”

玛丽答道：“我这就走，而且再也不会回来了！我本来想和你说说迪康和他的小动物的事，现在我不跟你说了。”

她跑出屋去，心里又生气又难过。现在她永远都不会告诉科林她的大秘密了。

回到自己房间后，她看到桌上有几本书。这些书是克雷文先生给她的礼物，有几本是图画书，有两本是园艺方面的书。

present
n. 礼物
gardening
n. 园艺

“克雷文先生多好啊。”她想道。接着她想起了科林，她开始为科林感到一点儿难过。“可怜的科林，”她想道，“也许他整个下午都在想着他的驼背，也许我明天该去看看他。”

她因为疲倦，早早就上床安歇，可是半夜里她突然醒了。外面一片骚动，有人在走廊里跑动，远远的还有人在哭。

“是科林”，她想道，“我不知道该怎么办，但是必须有人劝他别哭。”

玛莎忽然冲到她的屋里。“噢，玛丽，”她喊道，“请你让他别哭了！他会哭坏身体的。请你去让他别哭了！他喜欢你。”

于是玛丽就到科林的屋里去了。玛丽一见到他，就高声喊道：“别哭啦！别哭啦！别哭啦！你要是再

and I can make more noise than you can. I'll frighten you!"

Colin was so surprised that he almost stopped crying. No one had ever shouted at him before.

"I can't stop!" he cried. "I can't!"

"Yes, you can," Mary answered.

"I'm going to be a hunchback," he cried. "I know it! I felt my back, and it has changed."

"No, it hasn't. Don't be foolish," Mary said. "Let me see."

She looked at his back. It was very thin and weak, but it was quite straight, and she told him so.

"Of course you're not going to be a hunchback," she said loudly. "Your back is as good as mine."

Colin smiled weakly. He believed that Mary was **telling the truth**. "Do you think that I will live?" he asked her.

"Of course you'll live," she said. "But you'll have to go outside in the fresh air a great deal."

"I'll come with you," he said quietly.

"Now," said Mary, "you must go to sleep. Shall I sing to you again?"

"Will you tell me about the secret garden **instead**?" he asked her. "Have you found the key?"

"Yes, I think so," answered Mary. "I'll tell you about it tomorrow. Now go to sleep."

She held his hand, and sang very softly. He went to sleep very quickly.

哭，我也要哭了，我会哭得比你声音更大的。我会把你吓一大跳！”

科林大吃一惊，差点就不哭了。还从来没有人向他大喊大叫过。

“我止不住哭！”他哭喊道，“我止不住！”

“你能的”。玛丽说。

“我会成为驼背，”他哭道，“我知道的！我摸了脊背，它已经和以前不一样了。”

“没有，它没有变弯。别犯傻了，”玛丽说道，“让我看看。”

她看了科林的脊背，他的脊背很瘦弱，但是很直。她就把所看到的告诉他了。

“你当然不会成为驼背啦，”她高声说道，“你的脊背跟我的脊背一样直。”

tell the truth 说实话

科林有气无力地笑了，他相信玛丽说的是实话。“你说我会活下去吗？”他问玛丽。

“你当然会活下去，”她说，“可是你得常常到外面去呼吸新鲜空气。”

“我要和你一起去。”科林轻轻地说。

“现在你得睡觉了，”玛丽说道，“要不要我再给你唱歌啊？”

instead *adv.* 替代

“不如你给我说秘密花园的事，好吗？”他求她，“你找到花园的钥匙了吗？”

“我想我找到了，”玛丽回答道，“我明天再跟你谈这件事。现在睡觉吧。”

她握住科林的手，柔声唱了起来，科林很快就睡着了。

Language Points to Remember
好句好段记心上

1. But when she saw Martha, she knew that something was not right.
   可是她一看见玛莎，就知道出事了。
2. And they shouted at each other for some time.
   他们俩这样互相嚷嚷了好一会儿。
3. He believed that Mary was telling the truth.
   他相信玛丽说的是实话。

CHAPTER 17

Mary Tells Colin the Secret

玛丽把秘密告诉了科林

· QUESTIONS BEFORE READING ·

- Who was coming to see Colin the next day?
- What surprised Dr Craven when he saw Colin?

The next morning Mary slept late, because she was very tired. When Martha came in, she said: "Colin wants you to go to him as soon as you can. He seems to like you very much. I don't know why, because you were very angry with him last night." And she laughed. "He said, 'Please ask Mary to come.' I don't think he has ever said 'please' to anyone in his life before!"

Mary wanted very much to go to the secret garden, but she went to see Colin first.

"I'm glad you came," Colin said. "I feel very tired this morning. My **whole** body hurts. What are we going to do today?"

"Well," said Mary slowly. "First, I'm going to see Dickon, but I'll come back soon," she added quickly, because Colin looked so sad. "And when I come back, I'll tell you something very important—it's about the secret garden."

"Oh, how wonderful!" cried Colin. "Please come back quickly."

Mary went out into the garden, and Dickon was there before her again.

Every day now there were more things alive in the garden.

第二天早上玛丽睡了个懒觉，因为她太累了。玛莎进来时，告诉她说："科林要你尽快去见他，他好像很喜欢你。我不知道这是为什么，其实昨天夜里你对他很凶啊。"玛莎说着笑了，"他说，'请叫玛丽来。'我想他以前从来没有对谁说过一个'请'字！"

玛丽很想到秘密花园里去，可是她还是先去看了科林。

"我很高兴你来了，"科林说道，"我今天早上感到很疲倦，我全身都痛。咱们今天干什么好呢？"

whole
adj. 整个

"嗯，"玛丽慢慢地说道，"首先，我要去见迪康，可是我很快就会回来。"玛丽赶紧接着说，因为科林看上去很伤心，"等到我回来以后，我会告诉你一件非常重要的事——是关于那秘密花园的事。"

"噢，太棒了！"科林喊道，"请你快去快回。"

玛丽出去到花园去了，迪康又是比她早到那里。

现在每天花园里都有更多的花草树木苏醒过来，

It was like magic. Mary and Dickon sat down, and she told him what had **happened** during the night. Then she told him that Colin wanted to see him and his animals. Dickon thought that this was a good plan, and he said he would come the next day.

The garden was so beautiful that Mary did not want to go back to Colin, but she did. And Colin looked very pleased to see her again.

She sat down and they talked about Dickon and his animals.

"Do they really understand what Dickon says?" asked Colin. "And does he really know what they say to him?"

"He says he does," Mary answered. "He says that anyone can understand an animal, although they must be one of the animal's friends."

"I wish I had friends," said Colin sadly. "But I don't like people, and people don't like me."

"Don't you like me?" Mary asked him.

"Yes," he said, and he **sounded** surprised.

"Ben Weatherstaff once told me that I was like him," Mary said. "He said, 'We don't look nice and friendly, and I don't think that we are!' Perhaps you are the same. But," she stopped to think, "I think that I am nicer now that I know the robin and Dickon."

"Mary," said Colin quietly, "I'm sorry that I said those unkind things about Dickon yesterday. I hated him because you liked him, but I made a mistake. I do want to see him very much."

happen
v. 发生

sound
v. 听起来

就像魔法一样。玛丽和迪康坐下来，对他说了昨天夜里发生的事。然后她又告诉迪康说科林想见他和他的小动物们。迪康觉得这个主意很好，他说他第二天会来的。

花园太美了，玛丽都不想回到科林那儿去，可是她还是去了。科林看见她回来，显得很高兴。

她坐下来，两个人谈着迪康和他的小动物们。

“那些动物真的听得懂迪康说的话吗？”科林问道，“迪康也真的听得懂动物们吗？”

“他说他听得懂，”玛丽回答说，“他说谁都听得懂动物的话，只不过必须和动物交朋友。”

“但愿我有朋友，”科林伤心地说，“可是我不喜欢别人，别人也不喜欢我。”

“你难道不喜欢我吗？”玛丽问他道。

“我喜欢你。”他说道，他听来很惊讶。

“本·韦瑟斯塔夫有一回告诉我说我很像他，”玛丽说，“他说：‘我们看来不友善，而且我想我们的确不友善！’也许你也是这种人。但是，”她停下来想了想，“我想我自从认识那知更鸟和迪康以后好多了。”

“玛丽，”科林静静地说，“我很抱歉昨天说了迪康那么多坏话。因为你喜欢他，所以我恨他。但是我错了，我确实很想见他。”

"I'm glad that you said that," Mary answered, "because . . . because . . . " she stopped. "Can you keep a secret? Can you really keep a secret?"

"Yes, yes," Colin cried.

"Well," said Mary, "Dickon will come to see you tomorrow and he'll bring his animals with him." Colin's eyes grew bigger and bigger. "But that isn't everything," she said. "Listen. This is better. There is a door to the secret garden, and I have found the key."

Colin could not believe it. "Will I see it?" he cried.

"Of course you'll see it," Mary answered. And then she told him what the garden was really like.

Later that day Dr Craven came to see Colin. Mrs Medlock had told him what had happened during the night, so he was very surprised that Colin was not in bed.

"I'm sorry that you were ill last night, Colin," he said.

"I'm much better now," Colin answered. Again Mary thought of the Indian prince. "I want to go outside," he went on. "I want some fresh air."

"You must be very careful," said Dr Craven. "I thought that you didn't like fresh air."

"I don't when I'm alone," Colin answered. "But Mary is going to come with me. Dickon is going to push my wheelchair. We will go alone."

Dr Craven did not like this plan. He thought that it might make Colin ill again, but he could not stop the boy. He left the room, and he could not believe what he had seen.

“我很高兴你这样说了，”玛丽答道，“因为……因为……”她住了口，“你能保守秘密吗？你真能保守秘密吗？”

“我能，我能！”科林喊道。

“好吧，”玛丽说，“迪康明天会来见你，他还会把他的动物们都带来。”科林的眼睛越瞪越大。“可是还不只是这一件事，”她说道，“听着，还有更好的事呢。那秘密花园有一扇门，而且我已找到了钥匙。”

科林无法相信。“能让我看看吗？”他喊。

“你当然能看，”玛丽答道。然后她就告诉他那花园究竟是什么样子的。

那天晚些时候，克雷文医生来看科林了。梅德洛克太太已经告诉他那天夜里发生的事，所以看见科林居然没有卧床，他很惊讶。

他说：“科林，我很抱歉昨天夜里你又犯病了。”

“我现在好多了。”科林回答道。玛丽又想起了那位印度王子。“我想要到外面去，”他接着说，“我要呼吸些新鲜空气。”

“你可得万分小心，”克雷文医生说，“我本以为你不会喜欢新鲜空气的。”

“我独自一人时是不喜欢的。”科林答道，“但是玛丽会陪着我去，迪康会给我推轮椅，就我们三个。”

克雷文医生不喜欢这个主意，他认为这可能会使科林再次犯病，但是他无法阻止他。他出去了，很难相信自己看到的一切。

Language Points to Remember
好句好段记心上

1. Mary wanted very much to go to the secret garden, but she went to see Colin first.
玛丽很想到秘密花园里去，可是她还是先去看了科林。

2. He says that anyone can understand an animal, although they must be one of the animal's friends.
他说谁都听得懂动物的话，只不过必须和动物交朋友。

3. There is a door to the secret garden, and I have found the key.
那秘密花园有一扇门，而且我已找到了钥匙。

CHAPTER 18
Colin Sees the Secret Garden at Last
科林终于看到了秘密花园

· Questions before Reading ·

- Why didn't Mary and Dickon want to talk about the broken tree? (Because . . .)
- Why did Colin stand against a tree?
- Who must know about the secret garden? (Only . . .)

They had to wait for a week, however, before Colin could go to the garden, because there were some very **windy** days, and then he caught a cold. But Dickon went to see Colin every day and told him what was happening outside.

At last Colin was outside. Dickon pushed the wheelchair, and Mary walked beside it. Colin looked up at the sky, and **breathed** the fresh air. His eyes grew bigger and bigger.

They saw no one in the gardens, but they walked around for a long time before they went into the secret garden.

"This is where the robin showed me the key," Mary said. "And this—this is the door. Push the wheelchair inside quickly, Dickon!" she cried.

Colin covered his eyes with his hands. He did not look until they were inside the garden. Then he looked at everything, in the same way that Mary and Dickon had done when they first saw the garden.

"I will get better!" he cried. "Mary and Dickon, I will get well! I will live for ever and ever!"

That afternoon Colin felt that the whole world was good

windy
adj. 多风的

breathe
v. 呼吸

然而，他们不得不等了一周科林才能去看秘密花园，因为有几天刮了大风，后来他又得了感冒。但是迪康每天都去看科林，告诉他外面发生了什么事。

科林终于出来了，迪康给他推着轮椅，玛丽在旁边走着。科林抬头看看天，呼吸着新鲜的空气，他的眼睛越睁越大。

尽管他们在菜园子一个人也没看见，他们还是转来转去走了好久才进了秘密花园。

“这就是那知更鸟领我找到钥匙的地方，”玛丽说道，“而这个——这个就是花园的门了。迪康，快把轮椅推进来！”她喊道。

科林用双手遮住眼睛，等进到花园里面才拿开手看。然后他把园里的一切都看了个遍，正像玛丽和迪康头一次看见花园时那样。

“我会好起来的！”他喊道，“玛丽、迪康，我会好起来的！我会永远、永远地活下去！”

那天下午科林觉得整个世界都美好无比。他开

and beautiful. He began to feel better and to look better. His face became less white, and he laughed all the time. He sat in his wheelchair under one of the fruit trees while Dickon and Mary worked. They brought him things to see. Then Dickon pushed the chair slowly around the garden, and they stopped and looked at all the wonderful things. Colin thought that the garden was like a fairy garden.

"I wonder if we will see the robin?" he asked Dickon. Then he noticed an old tree. "Why is part of that tree **broken**?" he asked.

"It happened a long time ago," Dickon answered. He stopped, and then he said suddenly: "Look, look, there's the robin."

So Colin saw the robin at last, and he forgot to ask about the broken tree. Mary and Dickon were very glad about this, because the broken tree had caused the death of his mother, and they did not want to tell him that.

"I don't want this afternoon to end," said Colin slowly. "But I'll come back tomorrow, and the day after and the day after that. I've seen the spring and now I want to see the summer. I want to grow with the garden."

"And you will," said Dickon. "You'll soon be able to walk and work and use a spade like Mary and me."

"Walk!" said Colin, very surprised. "Use a spade! Will I?"

"Of course," said Mary and Dickon together. "You've got legs, haven't you? We must make them strong."

始感觉好些了，也显得健康起来，他的脸不再那么苍白了，总是笑个不停。玛丽和迪康干活的时候，他在果树下，坐在轮椅里。他们拿了很多东西给他看，后来迪康推着轮椅在花园里慢慢转了一圈，每当有奇妙的东西时他们就停下来仔细看。科林认为这花园像是一座神仙的花园。

"不知道我们会不会看见那知更鸟？"他问迪康。然后他注意到一棵老树，"这树为什么断了一截？"

broken
adj. 损坏的，断裂的

"那是很久以前的事了。"迪康回答道。他住口不说了，然后忽然说道："看呀，看呀，知更鸟在那儿。"

这样科林终于看见了那知更鸟，也就忘了追问断树的事。玛丽和迪康对此很高兴，因为科林的母亲就是因为那棵断树才死去的，而他们俩不想告诉他这件事。

"我不想让这个下午过完。"科林慢慢说，"可是我明天还要到这里来，还有后天，还有大后天都要来。我已经见到了春天，现在我想看看夏天。我想和这花园一起长大。"

"你一定会的。"迪康说道，"你很快就能够像玛丽和我一样走路、干活、用铲子了。"

"走路！"科林极为惊讶地说道，"用铲子！我能行吗？"

"当然了。"玛丽和迪康一起说道，"你也有两条腿，不是吗？我们一定要让你的腿结实起来。"

It was nearly evening, and the sun was going down. The garden was very still and quiet.

Suddenly Colin said, "Who is that man?"

"Which man?" cried Mary and Dickon.

Colin **pointed to** the wall. Mary and Dickon turned, and there was Ben Weatherstaff. They could only see his head over the top of the wall. He looked very angry. From the place he had climbed to he could only see Mary.

"What are you doing, you bad girl?" he shouted.

"How did you get into that garden?"

"The robin **showed me the way**," Mary answered.

Dickon pushed Colin's wheelchair nearer Ben Weatherstaff, and when Ben saw Colin he looked and looked.

"Do you know who I am?" Colin asked him.

"Yes, I do," answered Ben, "because you look so like your mother. How did you get here? I thought you were a hunchback."

"I'm not a hunchback," said Colin loudly. "I'm not!"

"No, he's not!" Mary shouted too. "I've seen his back and he's not a hunchback."

"Come here!" Colin shouted to Dickon. "Come here at once!" And he started to stand up. Mary's face went white, because she was very frightened. She said quietly again and again. "He can do it! He can do it!" And Colin did. He held Dickon's arm; he put his thin legs on the ground; and suddenly he was standing up, with his head held high.

"Now—look at me, Ben Weatherstaff!" he shouted. "Am I a

临近傍晚，太阳要落山了。花园里很安静，没有响动。

科林忽然问道："那个人是谁？"

"哪个人？"玛丽和迪康同时叫道。

point to
指着

科林指着园墙，玛丽和迪康转过身去，看见是本·韦瑟斯塔夫。他们只能看见他的头露出墙头，他的样子非常愤怒。从他爬上去的地方只能看见玛丽一个人。

"你在干什么，你这个坏丫头？"他喊道，"你是怎么进到园里去的？"

show sb the way
给某人指路

"知更鸟给我带的路。"玛丽回答道。

迪康把科林的轮椅推到本·韦瑟斯塔夫近旁。本看见科林，就目不转睛地盯着他。

"你知道我是谁吗？"科林问他。

"是的，我知道，"本答道，"因为你太像你母亲了。你是怎么到这里来的？我本来以为你是个驼背呢。"

"我不是驼背，"科林高声说道，"我不是！"

"不，他不是！"玛丽也大声说，"我看见过他的背，他不是驼背。"

"过来！"科林向迪康喊道，"马上到这里来！"说着他就开始起身站立。玛丽的脸都白了，因为她很害怕。她反反复复小声地说："他能行！他能行！"科林果然能行。他抓住迪康的胳膊，把双脚放到地上，忽然间他站起来了，高扬着头。

"哼，你看着我，本·韦瑟斯塔夫！"他高声叫着，

hunchback?"

"No, no!" Ben answered, and Mary thought that she saw **tears** in the old man's eyes. "No—I can't believe it! Eh! People haven't told the truth about you, my boy. God **bless** you!"

Colin said, "Come here. Mary will show you the way. I want to talk to you. Be quick!"

Before Ben Weatherstaff came into the garden with Mary, Colin said to Dickon. "I can stand and now I'm going to walk to that tree. I will stand against it when Ben Weatherstaff comes."

He walked over to the tree.

When Ben came through the door, he could not believe what he saw.

"What work do you do in the gardens?" Colin asked him.

"Everything," Ben answered. "They give me work because your mother liked me, although I'm really too old now. This was her garden and she loved it."

"It's my garden now, and I love it, too," said Colin. "But it's a secret. No one must know about it—only Mary, Dickon, you and me."

Just then Colin noticed Mary's spade on the ground. He **picked** it **up**, and he began to work with it. He did not work very well, but he looked very happy.

"And now," he said, as he put the spade down, "I've walked and I've used a spade. You said that I would, Dick on, and I've done it!"

“我是驼背吗？”

“不，不是的！”本答道，玛丽觉得老人的眼里好像有泪花在闪，“不，我都不敢相信！嗐！孩子，大家都没说实话。上帝保佑你！”

tear
n. 眼泪
bless
v. 保佑

科林说：“进来吧。玛丽会给你带路的。我要和你谈一谈，快点！”

玛丽还没把本·韦瑟斯塔夫领进花园，科林就对迪康说：“我已经能站着了，现在我要走到那棵树那儿去。本·韦瑟斯塔夫来的时候我要靠着树站着。”

他走到了那棵树那里。

本·韦瑟斯塔夫从门里进来时，他都不敢相信自己的眼睛了。

“你在菜园子里干什么活？”科林问他。

“什么活都干，”本答道，“虽说我现在年纪太大了，他们还给我活干，因为你母亲喜欢我。这里原来是她的花园，她很喜欢它。”

“现在它是我的花园了，我也喜欢它。”科林说道，“可是这是个秘密，不能让任何人知道，只有玛丽、迪康、你和我知道。”

这时科林看到了地上玛丽的铲子。他把它拿了起来，开始干活，他干得并不太好，可是他看来很快乐。

pick up
捡起，拿起

“现在嘛，”他把铁铲放下说道，“我走过路了，也用过铁铲了。迪康，你说过我能行，现在我都干了！”

Language Points to Remember
好句好段记心上

1. Colin looked up at the sky, and **breathed** the fresh air. His eyes grew bigger and bigger.
   科林抬头看看天，呼吸着新鲜的空气，他的眼睛越睁越大。
2. Then Dickon pushed the chair slowly around the garden, and they stopped and looked at all the wonderful things.
   后来迪康推着轮椅在花园里慢慢转了一圈，每当有奇妙的东西时他们就停下来仔细看。
3. They could only see his head over the top of the wall.
   他们只能看见他的头露出墙头。
4. When Ben came through the door, he could not believe what he saw.
   本·韦瑟斯塔夫从门里进来时，他都不敢相信自己的眼睛了。

CHAPTER 19
Magic
魔　法

· Questions before Reading ·

- What was Dickon's mother's plan? (Every day . . .)
- What was the result? (Colin didn't . . .)

Dr Craven was waiting for them when they got back to the house.

"You have stayed outside too long," he said to Colin. "You must be more careful."

"But I'm not tired," answered Colin, "I feel better, and tomorrow I shall stay outside all day."

Dr Craven did not look pleased about this, but he knew that he could not stop Colin.

After he had gone, Mary said to Colin: "I feel sorry for Dr Craven."

"Why?" asked Colin. "Because he won't get Misselthwaite Manor?"

"No," answered Mary. "Because he must be nice to you, **although** you are **unkind** to him."

"Am I unkind?" asked Colin.

"Yes, you are," answered Mary. She was not being unkind herself; she wanted to tell Colin the truth. "No one has ever done anything that you didn't like because you were always ill."

"But I'm not ill now. I'm going to get better," he said. "And

他们回到宅子里时，克雷文医生在等着他们。

“你在外面待得太久了，”他对科林说，“你应当更小心些。”

“可是我不累，”科林答道，“我觉得好多了。明天我要在外面待一整天。”

克雷文医生对此好像并不高兴，但是他知道无法阻止科林。

他走了以后，玛丽对科林说：“我很可怜克雷文医生。”

“为什么？”科林问道，“是因为他得不到米瑟斯韦特庄园吗？”

“不是的，”玛丽回答说，“因为你虽然对他不友好，但他必须对你好。”

“我不友好吗？”科林问。

“是的，不友好。”玛丽回答说。她不是刻薄，而是她想对他实话实说：“谁也没有干过任何你不喜欢的事，就因为你一直在生病。”

“可是现在我没有病了，我会好起来，”科林说道，

although
conj. 即使
unkind
adj. 不仁慈的，不和善的，不客气的

I'm not going to be unkind again."

"Good," said Mary. "The garden and its magic will help you, because there is magic in the garden."

During the next few months there really was magic in the garden. The children went there every day, and as Colin grew stronger, the garden grew more and more beautiful. There were flowers everywhere, and the roses were wonderful. Colin watched each change **carefully**, and Dickon told him and Mary about the plants and flowers and the animals and the birds. Each day Colin worked and walked more. This was the real magic of the garden. It made Colin want to get better, and he did. One day he walked all around the garden. Mary and Dickon walked on each side of him; Ben Weatherstaff walked behind them and all Dickon's animals came at the end. They walked very slowly, and they stopped often, but Colin was very happy. "The magic is making me strong!" he cried. "The magic is in me!"

When he was back in his wheelchair under the tree he said, "I'm not going to tell Dr Craven that I'm better. This is to be the greatest secret of all. I'm not going to tell any one until I can run and walk like Dickon. I shall come here every day in my wheelchair. Then, when my father comes home, I shall walk into his room and say, 'Here I am. I'm very well and I'm going to live to be a man. The magic of the garden has helped me.'"

"He won't believe you," Mary said, and she laughed. "He'll think that he's asleep!"

There was one thing which was difficult for Colin now. He

“我不会再对别人不好了。”

“好极了，”玛丽说，“这花园和它的魔法会帮助你，因为这花园是有魔法的。”

其后的几个月里，花园真的现出魔法来。孩子们天天到那儿去，随着科林的身体日益强壮起来，花园变得越来越美。到处都是花儿，玫瑰花真是美妙极了。科林细心地观察着每一个变化，迪康向他和玛丽传授有关植物、花卉、动物和鸟类的知识。科林一天比一天走得多一些，干得多一些。这才是花园真正的魔力所在，这魔力使科林想变得更健康，他确实也健壮起来了。有一天他绕着整个花园走了一圈。玛丽和迪康在他两旁陪着，本·韦瑟斯塔夫走在他们后面，最后跟着的是迪康所有的小动物们。他们走得非常慢，又时常停下来，可是科林非常快乐。“那魔力正在使我强壮起来！”他欢呼道，“魔力就在我身体里！”

carefully
adv. 仔细地，小心地

他回到树下，坐到轮椅上，然后说道：“我不会告诉克雷文医生我身体好多了，这会是最大的秘密。等到我能和迪康一样又走又跑的时候，我再告诉别人。我每天都要坐着轮椅到这来，然后，等我父亲回来以后，我会自己走到他的房间里，对他说：‘我来了。我身体很好，我要活下去，成为男人。花园的魔力帮助了我。’”

“他不会相信你的，”玛丽说着笑了，“他会以为自己在做梦！”

现在有一件事使科林感到有点棘手，他老是觉

was hungry all the time. He was frightened that the servants might learn about his secret because he ate so much. It was strange that a **sick** boy could eat so much! Colin and his friends did not know what to do. But then Dickon told his mother, and she had a plan. Every day she gave Dickon fresh bread for Mary and Colin. After that Colin did not want to eat so much at meal times.

Poor Dr Craven! He did not know what to think. Before Colin went out into the gardens every day he ate nothing. Then, when he first went out, he ate much more. But now suddenly he did not eat again. It was very strange! But there was something even more strange—although Colin was not eating again, he was still growing fatter.

But no one learnt what the secret was. Colin told no one where they went, although Dr Craven often asked him. The three children were outside all day when it wasn't raining. Colin grew stronger and fatter all the time.

One day Colin said to Mary: "I wish my father would come home. I want to tell him the secret myself, but I think that the servants are going to learn about it soon. I'm getting quite fat, and I don't look the same. I wish that the magic would bring my father home."

sick
adj. 虚弱的，恶心的

得饿。他害怕佣人们会知道他的秘密，因为他吃得这么多。一个生病的孩子竟然吃得下这么多东西，这也太奇怪了！科林和他的小朋友们不知怎么办才好。后来迪康把这件事告诉了他的母亲，她想出了一个主意。她每天给迪康一些新鲜面包，带给玛丽和科林。从那以后，科林在吃饭的时候就不想吃那么多了。

可怜的克雷文医生！他颇费脑筋。科林每天去花园以前，他什么都不吃。后来，刚出去的时候，他吃得多了许多。现在，他忽然又不吃东西了。这真是太奇怪了！可是还有比这更奇怪的事，虽说科林又不肯吃东西了，他还是渐渐在变。

可是谁也没发现那个秘密，科林不告诉别人他们到哪儿去了，尽管克雷文医生常问他。只要不下雨，三个孩子整天到外面去。科林越长越强壮，越长越胖。

有一天科林对玛丽说："真希望我爸爸会回家来。我想亲自把秘密告诉他，可是我觉得仆人们很快就会知道这个秘密了。我长得相当胖了，样子都跟以前不一样了。但愿那魔力能够把我父亲带回家来。"

Language Points to Remember
好句好段记心上

1. Dr Craven did not look pleased about this, but he knew that he could not stop Colin.
   克雷文医生对此好像并不高兴，但是他知道无法阻止科林。

2. There were flowers everywhere, and the roses were wonderful.
   到处都是花儿，玫瑰花真是美妙极了。

3. But no one learnt what the secret was.
   可是谁也没发现那个秘密。

CHAPTER 20
Mary and Colin Meet Dickon's Mother

玛丽和科林见到迪康的母亲

· Questions before Reading ·

- What had happened to Colin in the secret garden?

  (He had grown . . .)
- What had happened to Mary?

One day, after it had rained for a week, Mary, Colin and Dickon were in the garden again, **working hard**, when suddenly Colin stopped.

"Mary, Dickon!" he cried. "Look at me! I'm really well at last! It's **real**. I'm well!" He had thought about it for such a long time, and now it was true. He felt very happy. "I will live for ever and ever!" he shouted. "Because the magic has helped me!"

Just then he looked towards the door of the garden.

"Who is that?" he asked. "Who is it?"

A woman was standing by the door. She had a very kind face, and she was laughing. Dickon ran across the grass. "It's mother!" he shouted, and Mary and Colin ran, too.

"I knew that you wanted to see her," said Dickon, "and so I told her where to find the door."

Colin was very happy. "I've always wanted to see you, Mrs Sowerby," he told her. "Even when I was ill. You and Dickon and the garden were the first things that I wanted to see in my whole life."

work hard
努力工作

real
adj. 真的，真正的；真实的

下了一个星期的雨以后，有一天，玛丽、科林和迪康又到花园里去了。他们正在用力干活，忽然科林住手了。

“玛丽、迪康！”他喊道，“你们瞧瞧我！我终于真的好了！真的。我身体好了！”他盼着身体康复已经太久了，现在终于梦想成真，他感到非常高兴。“我要永远，永远地活着！”他高声喊道，“因为魔力帮助了我！”

正巧在这时候，他向花园的门看了一眼。

“那是谁呀？”他问道，“是谁呀？”

园门旁边站着一个女子，她有一副和善的面孔，正笑着。迪康跑过草地。“是我母亲！”他高呼道，玛丽和科林也跑了过去。

“我知道你们想见到她，”迪康说，“所以我告诉她到哪里能找到花园门。”

科林很高兴。“我一直想见到你，索尔比太太，”他告诉她，“在我还病着的时候就这么想了。你和迪康以及这花园是我这辈子最想要见到的。”

Mrs Sowerby did not say anything. She just looked kindly at the three young faces around her.

"Are you surprised that I'm so well?" Colin asked her next.

"Yes, I am," she answered. "And I'm also surprised because you look so like your mother."

"Do you think my father will like me?" Colin asked her. He was very frightened that his father would not want to see him. He had seen his father so little in his life that he thought his father did not like him.

"I'm sure he will, Colin," she answered.

Ben Weatherstaff came into the garden just then.

"Well, Mrs Sowerby," he said. "What do you think of Colin? Hasn't he grown strong? I can't believe that two months ago his legs were **so** thin **that** he couldn't walk."

"I think he's wonderful," Dickon's mother said, and then she turned to Mary. "And you've grown strong and healthy, too, Mary. You're a **pretty** girl now. I'm sure that you're like your mother, too."

Then they showed Mrs Sowerby everything in the garden—every tree and plant that had come alive. Mary and Colin liked her very much. She was so kind and quiet.

At last Colin asked her: "Do you believe in magic?"

"Yes, I do," she answered. "There are many names for it, but I know what you mean."

Colin and Mary were very pleased when they heard this.

Mrs Sowerby had brought **a basket of** food with her. After

索尔比太太什么话也没有说，她只是温和地看着她旁边三张年轻的面孔。

“你是不是看到我身体这么好，感到很惊奇啊？”科林接着问她。

“是的，我很惊奇。”她回答道，“而且还令我感到惊奇的是，你是这么地像你的母亲。”

“你觉得我父亲会喜欢我吗？”科林问她。他很害怕他的父亲会不想看见他。他一生中见到父亲的机会很少，这让他觉得父亲并不喜欢他。

“我敢肯定他会喜欢你的，科林。”她答道。

这时候本·韦瑟斯塔夫走进了花园。

“嗯，索尔比太太。”他说，“你觉得科林怎么样？他挺结实吧？我很难相信两个月以前他的双腿还那么瘦弱，路也不会走。”

so . . . that . . .
如此……以至于……

“我想他真是棒极了。”迪康的母亲说道，然后她转向玛丽，“玛丽，你也变得健壮了，你现在成了个漂亮的姑娘了。我敢说你也长得像你的母亲。”

pretty
adj. 漂亮的

然后他们带着索尔比太太看花园里的一切，每一棵苏醒的花草树木。玛丽和科林非常喜欢她，她真是又善良，又温柔。

终于科林问她：“你相信有魔法吗？”

“我相信，”她答道，“魔法有许多不同的叫法，可是我明白你说的是什么。”

科林和玛丽听到她这么说，非常高兴。

a basket of
一篮子

索尔比太太带来了一篮子吃的，他们绕着花园

they had walked around the garden, they sat down under one of the fruit trees. They ate a great deal, and while they ate Mrs Sowerby told them many stories about her children, and the moor and Yorkshire. They laughed a great deal.

"Ssshhh!" Said Colin. "We mustn't make so much noise—someone might hear us. Oh, Mrs Sowerby, it's so difficult. When we're together we want to laugh all the time, and we mustn't." Then he said quietly: "Do you think that my father will come home soon?"

"Yes. He'll come home soon," she answered. "He must come home. He'll be very happy when he sees you, Colin."

Then they talked about other things. They made plans for a **visit** to Mrs Sowerby's house. And then, too soon, it was time for her to go, and for Colin and Mary to go back to the house. Before Dickon's mother left, Colin went and stood in front of her, and said: "I wish you were my mother as well as Dickon's."

Her face looked almost sad when he said this. She put her arms round him and said: "Dear Colin! Your father must come home soon! He must!"

里走了一圈，就在一棵果树下坐了下来。他们吃得很多，一边吃一边听着索尔比太太讲她孩子们的许多故事，还有关于那草甸子和约克郡的许多事。他们不停地笑。

“嘘……！”科林说，“我们千万不要弄出那么大的动静，有人会听见的。噢，索尔比太太，这太难办了。我们在一起的时候，老是想笑，可是我们又不能笑。”然后他轻声地说：“你说我父亲很快就会回来吗？”

“是的，他很快就会回来，”她答道，“他必须回家来。科林，他看见你的时候会很高兴。”

然后他们谈了别的事，他们为到索尔比太太家去做客定了一个计划。后来，时间过得太快了，她该回家了，科林和玛丽也该回到宅子里去了。迪康的母亲走之前，科林走过去站在她面前，说：“我真希望你不仅是迪康的母亲，也是我的母亲。”

visit
n. 拜访

听见科林这么说，她脸上的表情几站是悲伤的。她伸出双臂抱着科林说：“亲爱的科林！你的父亲肯定就要回家了！一定是的！”

Language Points to Remember
好句好段记心上

1. Just then he looked towards the door of the garden.
   正巧在这时候，他向花园的门看了一眼。

2. I can't believe that two months ago his legs were so thin that he couldn't walk.
   我很难相信两个月以前他的双腿还那么瘦弱，路也不会走。

3. When we're together we want to laugh all the time, and we mustn't.
   我们在一起的时候，老是想笑，可是我们又不能笑。

CHAPTER 21
In the Garden
在花园里

· Questions before Reading ·

- What had Mary learnt?
- Where was Colin's father when the letter arrived?
- Who ran out of the garden?

While Mary was at Misselthwaite Manor, she learnt something very important. She learnt not to think only about herself. Now she thought a great deal about Dickon and his animals, about the secret garden and about Colin. She probably did not know that she had changed, but after six months she was a much nicer child.

Colin changed in the same way. Before he met Mary, he had thought only about himself—about his illnesses, his hunchback, and his **sadness**. But when he met Mary and Dickon and visited the secret garden every day, he began to change.

While these changes were happening at Misselthwaite Manor, Colin's father was **travelling** in countries **far away** from England. He visited Sweden, Norway, Switzerland and Italy. He never stayed in one place for long, and he was always very sad. He thought only about his dead wife, his sick son, and his own sadness.

One day at the end of summer, he was in Italy. He was sitting in a quiet garden and he fell asleep. While he slept, he remembered his wife. He thought he could hear her calling to

玛丽在米瑟斯韦特庄园里的时候，学会了一件非常重要的事。她学会了不该只想到自己。现在她常常想到迪康和他的动物们，想到秘密花园和科林。她很可能并未意识到自己已经变了，可是仅仅半年之后，她已变成一个可爱的女孩子了。

科林也发生着同样的变化。遇到玛丽以前，他想的只是他自己——自己的病，自己的驼背，自己的忧伤。可是自从他遇到了玛丽和迪康，并且每天都去秘密花园，他也开始变了。

当米瑟斯韦特庄园里发生着这些变化时，科林的父亲正在远离英格兰的各国旅行。他去了瑞典、挪威、瑞士和意大利。他在每个地方都待不久，而且总是感到哀伤。他只想到他死去的妻子、生病的儿子和自己的悲伤。

夏末的一天，他正在意大利。他坐在一个安静的花园里睡着了。在睡梦中他记起了他的妻子，他觉得仿佛听见她在呼唤他。

sadness
n. 悲伤，悲痛，凄惨

travel
v. 旅行
far away
遥远

him.

"Where are you, my dear?" he asked.

"I'm in the garden—in the garden," she answered.

Soon after, he woke up, and later he walked back to the house where he was staying. There was a letter for him. He opened it, and this is what it said:

Dear Mr Craven,

I hope that you will not be angry because I have written to you. You must come home to Misselthwaite Manor. Please Mr Craven, it is very important. Please come back as soon as possible.

Yours sincerely,
Susan Sowerby.

Mr Craven read the letter **twice**. "I will go back to Misselthwaite. I'll go now," he said.

A few days later he was back in Yorkshire. He began to feel happier, but he did not know why. During the journey he thought a great deal about Colin and about Mrs Sowerby's letter. He wondered why she had written to him. He did not know her very well, but he knew that she was a kind woman and a good mother. What was so important? Then he remembered what his wife had said while he was sleeping in the quiet garden in Italy.

As soon as he reached Misselthwaite Manor, he saw Mrs Medlock. His first question was. "How is Colin, Mrs Medlock?"

“你在哪儿，亲爱的？”他问。

“我在花园里，在花园里。”她答道。

他很快就醒了，稍后他走回他待的那所房子里。有他一封信，他拆开信，信里是这样说的：

亲爱的克雷文先生，

我希望你不会因为我给你写信而生气。你必须回家来，回到米瑟斯韦特庄园。求求你，克雷文先生，这是件要紧的事。请你务必尽快回来。

你诚挚的

苏珊·索尔比

twice
adv. 二次

克雷文先生把这封信读了两遍。“我要回米瑟斯韦特去，我现在就回去。”他说道。

几天以后他就回到了约克郡，他觉得高兴起来，可是他并不明白这是为什么。回来的路上，他时常想起科林，反复思忖索尔比太太的那封信。他纳闷她怎么会给他写信。他和她并不很熟，但是他知道她是一个善良的女人，是一位好母亲。有什么事情这么重要？接着他记起他在意大利那个安静的花园里睡着时，听见妻子说的话。

他一回到米瑟斯韦特庄园，就看见了梅德洛克太太。他马上问道：“梅德洛克太太，科林身体好吗？”

"Well, Mr Craven," she answered slowly, "he's . . . he's not the same."

"Is he still sick?" Mr Craven asked.

"Well . . . we don't know," Mrs Medlock answered.

"Why not?"

"Well . . . he's getting fatter, but he doesn't eat anything. He seems to be happier, and he even laughs with Mary Lennox and Dickon Sowerby. But he's **the same as** ever with Dr Craven and me."

"Where is he now?" Mr Craven asked.

"In the garden," Mrs Medlock answered.

"In the garden!" Mr Craven cried. "In the garden!" Those were the words that his wife had said to him in his sleep.

He went out into the gardens. He walked slowly, because he was thinking about the ten years since his wife's death. He wondered why he was going back to her garden after so many years. When he got to the place where he had hidden the key, he stopped.

"How strange," he thought. "I can hear children's **voices**, and yet no one has been inside this garden for ten years."

The sounds grew clearer. They were laughing. Suddenly a boy came through the door. He was running so fast that he almost made Mr Craven **fall over**. He was a tall, good-looking boy with dark hair and big eyes. Mr Craven knew at once who he was.

"Who?. . . What?. . . Who?" he cried.

Mary was standing near Colin, and she heard him say:

“嗯，克雷文先生，”她迟疑地答道，“他……和以前不同了。”

“他还生着病吗？”克雷文先生问道。

“嗯……我们不知道。”梅德洛克太太答道。

“为什么不知道？”

“嗯……他胖起来了，可是他什么都不吃。他看起来高兴多了，甚至跟玛丽·伦诺克斯和迪康·索尔比有说有笑的，可是他对我和克雷文医生还是老样子。”

the same as
与……一致，与……相同的

“他现在在哪里？”克雷文先生问道。“在花园里。”梅德洛克太太说道。

“在花园里！”克雷文先生叫道，“在花园里！”在睡梦中，他妻子就是这么对他说的。

他出去到了园子里。他走得很慢，因为他在思考着他妻子亡故以来10年中的事。他也不知道他为什么在这么多年以后还要回到她的花园去。他走到自己藏钥匙的地方，突然站住了。

voice
n. 声音

“太奇怪了，”他暗自想着，“我听得见孩子们在说话，可是这10年来没有人进过这花园。”

那话音越来越清楚了，孩子们在笑。忽然间一个男孩子从门里出来。他跑得飞快，差点把克雷文先生撞一个跟头。他个子高高的，长得很帅气，深色的头发，大大的眼睛。克雷文先生马上就知道他是谁了。

fall over
摔倒，跌倒

“是谁？……怎么回事？……谁呀？”他惊呼道。

玛丽正站在科林身旁，她听见科林说：“父亲，

"Father, I'm Colin. Can you believe it?"

Mr Craven could only say quietly: "In the garden! In the garden!"

"Yes," said Colin. "I'm better because of the garden. The garden and Mary and Dickon and his animals—and the magic—made me better. No one knows I am better. It has been a secret. I wanted you to know first."

Mr Craven was so happy that he could not speak.

"Aren't you glad, father?" Colin asked him. "Aren't you glad? I'm going to live for ever and ever!"

The garden was very beautiful in the late summer. Mr Craven looked at everything.

"I thought it would be dead," he said.

"So did Mary," said Colin. "But it has come alive!"

They all sat under a tree, and Colin told the story of the secret garden. They laughed happily about the robin, and Ben Weatherstaff, and the garden and the secret.

At last Colin said: "It will not be a secret any more. The servants will be very frightened when they see me, but I am never going to sit in that wheelchair again. I will walk back to the house with you, father."

And he did. All the servants were watching as Mr Craven and his son walked back to the house together. Colin looked very happy and so did his father, and Colin looked as healthy as any boy in Yorkshire.

我是科林。你能相信吗?”

克雷文先生只是小声说:“在花园里!在花园里!”

“是的。”科林说,“因为那花园,我好多了。因为那花园、玛丽、迪康,还有他的小动物们,还有那魔法,我好了起来。谁也不知道我好了,这是个秘密,我要让你第一个知道。”

克雷文先生高兴得说不出话来。

“你不高兴吗,父亲?”科林问他,“你不高兴吗?我要永远、永远地活下去!”

花园在夏末非常美丽,克雷文先生看着一切。

“我还以为这个花园会枯死。”他说。

“玛丽也曾经这么想,”科林说,“但它复苏了!”

他们都坐到一棵树下,科林讲述了秘密花园的故事。他们谈到那知更鸟、本·韦瑟斯塔夫,谈到花园和秘密,都高兴地笑了。

最后科林说:“这再也不是个秘密了。仆人们看见我会吓大跳,可是我再也不会坐那个轮椅了。我要和你一起走回宅子里去,父亲。”

他确实这样做了。所有的仆人都看着克雷文先生和他的儿子走着回到宅子里。科林看起来非常高兴,他的父亲也一样,而科林看起来和约克郡的其他的男孩一样健康。

Language Points to Remember
好句好段记心上

1. She probably did not know that she had changed, but after six months she was a much nicer child.
   她很可能并未意识到自己已经变了，可是仅仅半年之后，她已变成一个可爱的女孩子了。

2. He wondered why she had written to him.
   他纳闷她怎么会给他写信。

3. The sounds grew clearer.
   那话音越来越清楚了。

4. They all sat under a tree, and Colin told the story of the secret garden.
   他们都坐到一棵树下，科林讲述了秘密花园的故事。

Questions on the Whole Story

These are harder questions. Read the Introduction and think hard about the questions before you answer them. Some of them ask for your opinion, and there is no fixed answer.

1 Mary was "not at all a nice child" in India. Can you finish these sentences?

a Perhaps that was because her mother . . .

b Perhaps it was because the servants . . .

2 Martha:

a How did she show kindness to Mary?

b What did Mary learn from her about the moor, and about outdoor life?

c Who were Martha's favourite people?

3 Dickon:

a He loved animals, and they loved him. Can you give examples?

b What did he teach Mary?

4 Mrs Sowerby:

a What did Mary know about her before she met her?

b Why did she write to Mr Craven?

5 Colin:

a At first he was like Mary in some ways. What were they?

b Why was he so unhappy? Can you finish these sentences?

1 Because his father . . .

2 Because he thought . . .

3 Because no one . . .

c What do you think was really the "magic" that made him well?

6 Mr Craven:

a What is the "happy ending" to the story for him?

b Why was he so unhappy before that?

c Is it right for him to have a happy ending? Why?

朗文经典

读名著 学英语

- 第一级 1000词汇量
  1. *Five Famous Fairy Tales* 《著名童话五则》
  2. *Tales from Hans Andersen* 《安徒生童话》
  3. *Alice in Wonderland* 《爱丽丝奇遇记》
  4. *Robin Hood* 《罗宾汉》
  5. *The Prince and the Pauper* 《王子与贫儿》
  6. *Tales from the Arabian Nights* 《一千零一夜》
- 第二级 1200词汇量
  7. *King Arthur and the Knights of the Round Table* 《亚瑟王与圆桌骑士》
  8. *Adventures of Sindbad Sailor* 《辛巴达历险记》
  9. *Robinson Crusoe* 《鲁滨逊漂流记》
  10. *Gulliver's Travels* 《格列佛游记》
  11. *Round the World in Eighty Days* 《八十天环游世界》
  12. *The Three Musketeers* 《三个火枪手》
- 第三级 1500词汇量
  13. *A Christmas Carol* 《圣诞颂歌》
  14. *The Jungle Book* 《丛林故事》
  15. *The Mysterious Island* 《神秘岛》
  16. *Black Beauty* 《黑骏马》
  17. *Heidi* 《海蒂》
  18. *Three Adventures of Sherlock Holmes* 《福尔摩斯探案三故事》
- 第四级 1800词汇量
  19. *The Wind in the Willows* 《杨柳风》
  20. *A Tale of Two Cities* 《双城记》
  21. *Kidnapped* 《绑架》
  22. *Dracula* 《嗜血幽灵——德拉库拉》
  23. *The Secret Garden* 《秘密花园》

- 第五级　2000词汇量
  24. *Rip van Winkle and Other Stories*　《瑞普·范·温克尔》
  25. *The Return of Sherlock Holmes*　《福尔摩斯探案之归来记》
  26. *The Adventures of Tom Sawyer*　《汤姆·索耶历险记》
  27. *Vanity Fair*　《名利场》
  28. *The Swiss Family Robinson*　《海角一乐园》
- 第六级　2200词汇量
  29. *Stories from Shakespeare*　《莎士比亚戏剧故事》
  30. *Frankenstein*　《弗兰肯斯坦》
  31. *The Young King and Other Stories*　《少年国王》
  32. *The Count of Monte Cristo*　《基督山伯爵》
  33. *Little Women*　《小妇人》
- 第七级　2500词汇量
  34. *The Canterbury Tales*　《坎特伯雷故事集》
  35. *Three Great Plays of Shakespeare*　《莎士比亚三大戏剧故事》
  36. *David Copperfield*　《大卫·科波菲尔》
  37. *Tales of Mystery and Imagination*　《神秘及幻想故事集》
  38. *Oliver Twist*　《雾都孤儿》
- 第八级　2800词汇量
  39. *The Canterville Ghost and Other Stories*　《坎特维家的鬼魂》
  40. *The Adventures of Huckleberry Finn*　《哈克贝里·芬历险记》
  41. *Pride and Prejudice*　《傲慢与偏见》
  42. *King Solomon's Mines*　《所罗门王的宝藏》
  43. *Jane Eyre*　《简·爱》
- 第九级　3000词汇量
  44. *Dr Jekyll and Mr Hyde*　《化身博士》
  45. *The Call of the Wild*　《野性的呼唤》
  46. *Lorna Doone*　《洛娜·杜恩》
  47. *Wuthering Heights*　《呼啸山庄》
  48. *Treasure Island*　《金银岛》

轻松读名著，快乐学写作

——全国中小学生英文名著 Summary 写作大赛

熟读简易英文名著，学会用简单的词语表达丰富的意境！
无论是口语，还是写作，你的英文表达力都将一鸣惊人！

学习英语，就是为了掌握这种语言，并通过它去了解世界。沉浸在英语环境中是达到这一目的的捷径。对于非英语国家的学习者来说，阅读英语读物是进入英语环境最简便、最有效的方法。近年来，随着英语素质教育越来越受重视，教师、学生和家长都认识到进行大量原版英语阅读对于学好英语的重要性，国家教育部颁布的《英语课程标准》也对学生课外英语阅读提出了更高的标准和要求。著名英语专家、北京外国语大学教授钱青说，在我国当前外语学习环境还不够理想的情况下，仅靠精读接触的英语是不够的，还要通过阅读大量的原版作品来弥补，阅读简易读物是吸收新语言现象的最好途径。

有鉴于此，培生教育出版集团与中国对外翻译出版有限公司决定每年举办一次“轻松读名著，快乐学写作——全国中小学生英文名著Summary写作大赛”。Summary写作（摘要写作）是一种控制性的作文形式，它能使学生通过阅读原文，吸收原文的文章结构与语言方面的长处，写出内容一致、结构近似、语言简洁的短文。另外，对培养学生准确抓住文章重点的能力也有很大帮助，有利于他们在实际写作中避免面面俱到、事无巨细、一一罗列的不良倾向。这种写作既要准确理解原文，又要能综合概括；既能培养欣赏能力，又能训练书面表达能力。用英文写摘要，对学习英语写作的学生来说，是一种快捷、高效、实用的训练方法。

为配合此次写作大赛，培生教育出版集团和中国对外翻译出版有限公司精心甄选并出版了 48 本世界经典文学简易读本——“朗文经典·读名著　学英语”系列。这套丛书将为爱读书的你创造一个地道、丰富的英语环境，为你插上思维和语言的翅膀！当然，畅游过这些世界经典文学名著之后，别忘了参加我们的英文名著 Summary 写作大赛，你将有机会获得丰厚的奖品和全新的锻炼自我、展现自我的舞台。

一、主办单位

培生教育出版集团

中国对外翻译出版有限公司

二、参赛资格

凡购买并通读“朗文经典·读名著　学英语”系列任何一本英文名著的学生均有资格报名参加比赛

三、稿件要求

1. 稿件以每人 5 篇为限，要求全部用英文撰写，字数在 800~1200 单词之间

2. 参赛稿件必须是所读文学名著的 Summary，超出此范围视为无效稿件

3. 参赛文章须连同参赛报名表（复印无效）一并寄给主办单位方为有效参赛作品；参赛作品须注明指导教师，并附参赛者英文个人简介一份

4. 比赛的部分获奖作品将视情况在媒体或网络上发表，或结集出版；故获奖作者均视为同意主办单位发表其作品，版权归中国对外翻

译出版有限公司所有

5. 参赛作品必须为参赛者原创，如有舞弊，一经查出立即取消参赛资格，并由当事人承担由此引起的一切后果

6. 参赛者所提交的稿件及相关材料恕不退还，请作者自留底稿

四、投稿方式 截稿日期为每年 10 月 31 日（以当地邮戳为准）；请在信封左下角标明“参赛”字样，过期稿件自动转入下一年度比赛。

邮寄地址：北京市西城区车公庄大街甲 4 号物华大厦 6 层(100044)

收 件 人：外语图书事业部

五、奖项设置 大赛设小学组、初中组、高中组三个级别，每个级别设五个奖项

一等奖 10 名，奖品为获奖证书 + 价值 800 元的精品图书

二等奖 30 名，奖品为获奖证书 + 价值 600 元的精品图书

三等奖 60 名，奖品为获奖证书 + 价值 300 元的精品图书

优秀组织奖 30 名，此奖项颁发给指导参赛人数最多的教师，奖品为获奖证书 + 价值 500 元的精品图书

优秀指导奖 40 名，此奖项颁发给荣获一、二等奖参赛学生的指导教师，奖品为获奖证书 + 价值 500 元的精品图书

除获奖证书和图书奖品外，主办单位还将向获奖学生及指导教师所在的学校或班级寄发喜报。

六、获奖公布 所有获奖者名单将于每年 12 月 31 日刊登在中国对外翻译出版有限公司网站（www.ctpc.com.cn, www.aitbook.com)，欢迎登陆查询，同时主办单位将电话或 E-mail 通知所有获奖者。

七、大赛主办方拥有此次活动的最终解释权

参赛报名表

阅读作品			
参赛作品			
参赛选手		联系电话	
学校班级			
电子邮件			
通讯地址			
指导教师		联系电话	
电子邮件			
通讯地址			
作者声明：参赛作品为本人原创，不存在任何舞弊和抄袭行为。			
选手签字		教师签字	
本表格复印无效，表内各项信息务必填写完整、准确。			

本大赛最终解释权归中国对外翻译出版有限公司所有。